Table of Contents

Acknowledgements

When I curate an exhibition, I am looking for artists or artworks that offer something unexpected and surprising. I look for something that refuses to leave my head—and not necessarily because I like it. I approached *Now You See It* differently from what has usually defined my practice. I still wanted that same quality from all of the artworks included, but the basis for determining the content and purpose of the exhibition was different. Not only did I allow myself to sit with the exhibition concept for a substantially longer period of time, but I also talked over the ideas extensively with a wide variety of people whom I respect.

Now You See It celebrates uncertainty. A willingness to embrace doubt was inspired by several colleagues who are simultaneously pursuing very different but perhaps somehow philosophically linked exhibitions: Peter Eleey of the Walker Art Center and his exhibition *The Quick and The Dead*, Massimilliano Gioni of the New Museum and his exhibition *After Nature*, and Anthony Huberman of the Contemporary Art Museum St. Louis and his dual solo exhibitions of Gedi Sibony and Bruce Nauman. It is through a substantial number of emails and conversations with Eleey that many of the ideas of this exhibition and book were debated and clarified. I am grateful for his intellectual generosity and for the essay that he agreed to contribute.

Descending the stairs at the New Museum and encountering the Tino Seghal work—a woman writhing on the ground—in Gioni's exhibition was a significant art experience. I am excited about his public talk that will occur in Aspen just before the close of the show here. Huberman's perspective on knowing what one stands for as a curator, as well as his investment in questioning, has had an impact on my thinking.

After sharing with Jeremy Sigler, a poet and associate editor of *Parkett*, what I was working on and thinking about, he graciously shared a poem with me, which he had written earlier that day, and which we both agree seemed uncannily relevant. I am grateful for the poems he wrote specifically for this catalogue. And as I sat with George Stranahan, a man with incredibly varied and impressive accomplishments that range from founding the Aspen Center for Physics to creating and distributing beer and whiskey worldwide to being an accomplished photographer, it occurred to me that the phenomenon that I am pursuing in art with *Now You See It* must exist in other fields as well.

I am also grateful for the permission to reprint insightful thoughts on the very nature of art by Felix Gonzalez-Torres from an interview with Tim Rollins that was originally published by Art Resources Transfer in 1993. Paul Valéry's quote, "Seeing is forgetting the name of the thing one sees," was popularized as the title of Lawrence Weschler's seminal text on Robert Irwin. I am thrilled to be able to include here the extended text from which this quote is taken, translated for the first time into English, as it addresses many of the concerns I hope to highlight.

I would like to thank the following lenders to the exhibition for their belief in our program and willingness to support our efforts: 303 Gallery, New York; Baltimore Museum of Art; Yves Behar; Frances Dittmer; Martin and Rebecca Eisenberg; Esther Schipper, Berlin; Jack Hanley; Warren and Allison Kanders; Karyn Lovegrove Gallery; Jeanne and Michael Klein; Lisson Gallery, London; Robert and Nancy Magoon; MARC FOXX, Los Angeles; Marianne Boesky Gallery, New York; Susan and Larry Marx; Miller Meigs; Museum of Modern Art, New York; Debra and Dennis Scholl; Shane Cambell Gallery, Chicago; Siegelaub Collection & Archives at the Stichting Egress Foundation, Amsterdam; Laura Steinberg and B. Nadal–Ginard; Wallspace, New York; Ira G. Wool and Barbara Mirecki; Jann and Kenneth Williams; and Zwirner & Wirth, New York.

I am deeply grateful for the time and efforts of the following individuals and organizations to help secure works of art or their photographic images: Simone Montemurno of 303 Gallery; Cristin O'Keefe Aptowicz of The Artists Rights Society; Dr. Dirk Dobke of the Dieter Roth Foundation; Cynthia Daignault of The Felix Gonzalez-Torres Foundation; Michelle Pobar of Gagosian Gallery; Miciah Hussey and Gregg Deering of Gladstone Gallery; Alexandra Tuttle of Greene Naftali Gallery; Ashley Bellouin and Ava Jancar of Jack Hanley Gallery; Jennifer Smith of J Whitley Smith Consulting; Tim Buggs of Karyn Lovegrove Gallery; Sam Tsao of Friedrich Petzel Gallery; Heather Palmer and Lauren Staub of PaceWildenstein; Heather Rasmussen of Shane Campbell Gallery, Chicago; and Jane Hait of Wallspace, New York.

I would also like to thank Jared Rippy, Aspen Art Museum Graphic Designer, for his thoughtful design of this catalogue and all related exhibition graphics.

I wish to thank my colleagues at the Aspen Art Museum: Visitor Services Assistant Dasa Bausova, Chief Preparator and Facilities Manager Dale Benson, Campaign Coordinator Grace Brooks, Membership Assistant Ellie Closuit, Assistant Director for Finance and Administration Dara Coder, Curatorial Associate Nicole Kinsler, Education Assistant Giselle Leal, Executive Assistant to the Director Lauren Lively, Public Relations and Marketing Manager Jeff Murcko, Graphic Designer Jared Rippy, Web and Graphic Design Associate Rachel Rippy, Assistant Development Director Christy Sauer, Assistant Director for External Affairs John-Paul Schaefer, Visitor Services Coordinator Dorie Shellenbergar, Registrar and Exhibitions Manager Pam Taylor, Associate Curator Matthew Thompson, Special Events Assistant Wendy Wilhelm, and Staff Photographer Karl Wolfgang. I am extremely grateful to work with each and every one of you and proud of all that we are able to accomplish collectively.

We are deeply grateful for the financial assistance of our National Council. One hundred percent of its contributions go to support our exhibitions. The public programs presented on the occasion of the exhibition are part of the Questrom Lecture Series. Susan and Larry Marx's extremely generous support was vital to the realization of this exhibition, for which I am grateful.

Heidi Zuckerman Jacobson
Director and Chief Curator

Pay Attention Mother Fuckers

"I once was lost, but now am found,
Was blind, but now I see."[1]

At their best, people and works of art allow a reprieve from the blindness with which we traditionally see our world. When the white blindness that has afflicted all of the characters except the doctor's wife in José Saramago's novel *Blindness* finally abates, she reasons, "Why did we become blind, I don't know, perhaps one day we'll find out, Do you want me to tell you what I think, Yes, do, I don't think we did go blind, I think we are blind, Blind but seeing, Blind people who can see, but do not see."[2] What is the root cause of the blindness in Saramago's book? For his characters it is endemic. It affects all but one of them. The one who can see is left to witness the acts of the others. Unbeknownst to them, she becomes not only their sight, but also the recorder of their actions, the consciousness of the collective. Literary scholars have suggested that the blindness is in fact of a pathology or failure of consciousness. Saramago illustrates how quickly society breaks down when the ability to see beyond the tangible vanishes and hope abates. The metaphor resonates today, asking why—and what—can we not see?

Ad Reinhardt said, "The boundaries of seeing, like the perceptible aspects of nature or outer space, seem to extend as indefinitely as man's experience and experiments can take them. Art teaches people how to see."[3] Reinhardt's *Black Paintings* seem at first to be vast fields of pure blackness. Their apparent absence of pictorial interest challenges the dismissive assumptions of the traditional art viewer. If, however, the viewer looks harder and longer than they might initially feel compelled, sometimes subtle grids or other shades of color appear.[4] Standing and peering deep into the frame, allowing oneself to be comfortable with the blackness, facilitates a glimpse into the dark depths of one's soul and access to the space of fear, unknowing, and death. The *Black Paintings* offer perspective on the longevity of vision, commitment to seeing, and opportunity to transcend the immediate. They reward the persistent. Their magnificence is, however, often overlooked by viewers too quick, skeptical, or blind to see.

Ad Reinhardt, *Abstract Painting,* 1960 - 1966

That Reinhardt's paintings—absent of imagery—are elevated to the status of art can also arouse suspicion. From the adoption of the readymade by Marcel Duchamp to contemporary performances by Tino Seghal, it is understandable that many people feel as if they are being duped as claims of transcendence are made for these relatively unassuming aesthetic acts. Walter Benjamin wrote about the "aura" of works of art, how they can be imbued with an animate energy. When General Colin Powell endorsed Senator Barack Obama for the presidency, he cited the latter's "transformational quality," an ability to excite change heretofore unimagined. That magic is attracting. It dissipates skepticism and breeds hope.

The embodied magic of the artworks included in *Now You See It* counters the condition of blindness. When something stops being what it was before—dust, string, felt, even looking—and becomes something else, becomes art. A fissure forms.

Now You See It draws upon unconventional notions of transformation—like alchemy and magic—as a way of understanding this process as more than simply an elevation of base materials. As viewers, we hope for magic, against its impossibility. Yet, of course, it occurs. We know that human perception is a jerry-rigged apparatus, full of gaps, easily manipulated. People have a pronounced tendency to miss things that are happening right in front of them. We do not take in our surroundings so much as actively and constantly construct them. At a major conference in Las Vegas last year, psychologists argued that magicians have been engaging in cutting-edge, if informal, research into how we see and comprehend the world around us,[5] and that a better understanding of magicians and their techniques could offer insight into the behavioral and neural basis of consciousness itself.[6]

There is a particular kind of experience that is provoked by aesthetic indeterminacy around material appearance. *Now You See It* is about the magical moment of transformation and what happens to the viewer in the presence of such uncertainty. The viewer may experience something and nothing, dismissal and hope, epiphany and failure.

Some people believe only in the tactile, the here and now, and that any sort of "now you don't" is pure illusion. Others believe in the ability to know the unseen. The search for something outside our immediate reality extends across time and belief. In an essay on shamanist magic, writer Michael Taussig acknowledges that "the real skill of the practitioner lies not in skilled concealment but in the skilled revelation of skilled concealment. . . . Hence, power flows not from masking but from an unmasking which masks more than masking does."[7] By letting the viewer in on the secret, the magic of the secret is further reinforced. This magical transformation occurs simultaneously across visuality and consciousness. What you see morphs, by an alchemical process of visuality, into something more than it was initially.

Visibility and visual recognition are intimately connected to our understanding of an object's materiality. But how do we know what an object "is," of what it is really made? Although this question is often posed as a struggle between content and form, *Now You See It* features work that forces us to reexamine our basic assumptions about how we interpret the essence of an artwork's materials. Ralph Rugoff wrote that "art . . . ultimately exists through our thought and reflection, and in the unseen spaces that we carry within us. [A]rt . . . lives on in the uses we make of it—a potentially endless process by which, conceivably, we can alter the ways we see the world and shape the world we see."[8] Addressing temporality, immediacy, and perception, *Now You See It* is an exhibition about absence and presence, being and nothingness, simultaneous duality, literalism, the thing as itself and something else altogether.

Wade Guyton's untitled Epson UltraChrome inkjet on linen works are the contemporary equivalent of Reinhardt's *Black Paintings*. Their large, human scale creates a dark plane of space into which the viewer can visually meld. The works seem to be created almost as if by mistake. The mechanically produced "paintings" are made with a computer printer that allows the ink to build, leak, and get dragged and tracked across the linen.[9] Presented with more of this overwhelming blackness, accidentally created, the viewer has an opportunity to see the choice of blindness itself as the mistake.

In Saramago's text, the blindness was white, rather then black. Known for making white paintings, Robert Ryman's works can be seem as a rejoinder to the blackness of Reinhardt and Guyton. A substantial portion of *Now You See It* examines the use of particular mediums scaled back to their basic qualities. Ryman presents paint as paint, exploring the materials and properties of what makes a painting a painting.[10] The artist asks: how are paintings made, what are they made of, how are they installed in gallery and museum spaces, and how are these works experienced by those who encounter them? He exploits and explores a selective range of paintings' inherent and contextual qualities, including surface, support, medium, placement before the viewer, and, importantly, color, to gain the answers.[11] Ryman's paintings reveal their making. He often makes the hanging systems of his works visible and significant, extending his creative exploration beyond the edges of the picture plane. The metal fasteners and Scotch tape he uses serve both a practical and an aesthetic purpose, linking the paintings to the rest of the world and challenging traditional notions of the frame and pictorial space.[12] By extending the paintings into the realm of the viewer, they impact and affect that space. If the pictorial space expands infinitely, does art thereby consequently, and hopefully positively, impact the social space of life?

Light can also be blinding. The entire photographic process depends on light, and Walead Beshty captures its essence magnificently. His photographs depict their own making, revealing the magic of their creation. Beshty folds up photographic paper and exposes it to light. The paper is then unfolded and processed, creating abstract planes of color (or darkness) intersecting with blankness. The white spaces literally illustrate the void into which the light failed to travel.

Gedi Sibony has been termed "an alchemist of the everyday."[13] He takes seemingly valueless domestic construction materials and transforms them into something else, something sometimes aesthetic, sometimes surprising, sometimes magical. Sibony works with carpet, garbage bags, foam insulation, MDF, hollow-core doors, sticks, and levelor blinds. Many are castoffs, chosen for their familiarity and ubiquity, and patched together into haphazard forms.[14] Despite the beauty and seduction of the resulting objects, inherent in the work is the impossibility of actual transformation. You hope what you see is more than what it actually is. You believe that objects assembled by someone with a specific intention can cause a transformation, an imbuing of aura into something culled from the mundane. You hope all of this while acknowledging that it probably will not, probably can not. But, still, there is an open ended question, a maybe. How great it would be, that possibility to be conjured? As such, Sibony's work tests the limits of your faith in art, while simultaneously renewing it.[15]

As part of an ongoing interaction between artists Robert Morris and John Cage, the latter attempted to impress upon Morris the observation that "most of what happens never was in anybody's mind."[16] While Cage was comfortable with a reductive simplicity regarding the interaction between viewer and object, Morris needed to maintain a consciousness-based element to his work.[17] But the question of just where the consciousness is located is perhaps more compelling. Can it be located within the object, or just within the viewer? Is its presence important, or is it the *idea* of its presence that is important? Is the existence identified through its absence?

Morris's felt work *Vetti V* (1993) [page 33] cascades down the wall and pools on the floor, challenging the thick, structured fabric to flow elegantly with the quality of a wholly different substance. Peeled away at the center, the work reveals first gray, then pink, and suggests the interior of a feminine form, despite Morris's commitment to Minimalism's non-referential stance.

Lawrence Weiner has stated that art is about material objects. Many of the artists included in the exhibition are concerned with the role that art objects play in the world. Weiner has said, "Art, when it's placed into the context of the world, is not just used in the context of what we know as art history; it is an attempt to place material which could be used to enrich the daily lives of other human beings."[18] Weiner's *A 36" X 36" REMOVAL TO THE LATHING OR SUPPORT WALL OF PLASTER OR WALL BOARD FROM A WALL* (1968) [page 35] directly acknowledges the basis of visuality and art. The work is simply the removal of a square piece of a gallery wall, intended to reveal what is underneath. It is dumb geometry. The work is both humorous and insightful, addressing how and what we see, as well as what lies waiting to be seen just under the surface.

Fred Sandback has explained that when he began to use string, "I want[ed] to be able to make sculpture that didn't have an inside." He explored phenomenological geometry, adding, "I don't see various sculptures so much as being discrete objects. . . . The idea was to have the work right there along with everything else in the world. . . . It had utopian glimmerings of art and life happily cohabiting."[19] Because Sandback's sculptures are so visually subtle, the moment they appear to the viewer creates a fissure. The art has existed in the space of the viewer, unnoticed, until a precise moment. The accompanying recognition produces the moment of consciousness.

Ceal Floyer's witty conceptualism is manifested in exceedingly simple optical plays. In *Door* (1995) [page 39], Floyer points a slide projector at the base of an interior door, throwing a horizontal band of light along the bottom edge. The subtlety of the effect is that it appears as if the light is emanating from the other side rather then from superficial projection. In the video *Ink on Paper (video)* (1999) [page 41], the artist puts a marker to paper and lets all of the ink bleed out. The circle of ink radiates outward. The duration of the work is the amount of ink in the pen.

In a 1997 interview, Tom Friedman remarked, "I was thinking about how one's knowledge of the history behind something affects one's thinking about that thing." That year he completed *1,000 Hours of Staring* (1992–97) [page 43], in which he spent more than one thousand hours staring at a thirty-two-inch-square piece of white paper. Not only does he explore how the meaning of an ordinary object is transformed by contextual information,[20] but he creates a work of magical minimalism in which the viewer must ascertain the veracity of the object solely through his or her own system of belief. Perception—including the limits of our senses and how our brain is hardwired to make sense of our daily environment—is central to Friedman's practice.[21] Only once an object is placed in a gallery does it obtain significance. When that object is something not usually elevated as such, the viewer can come away puzzled. *Two by Four* (1990) [page 45] is a two-by-four, leaned against the wall, and painted to look exactly like itself. Its placement in the gallery, coupled with the trompe l'oeil finish, causes the viewer to pause. Floyer and Friedman both pursue a phenomenological dumbness.

Jennifer West exposes film to a variety of physical and chemical circumstances and encounters. The titles of her works hint at these processes, and they reveal the application of unusual materials to the emulsion. *Green M&M's & Mezcal Worm Film (70MM film leader with a mescal worm dragged over the surface—imprinted with hundreds of green M&M's)* (2008) [page 49] projects an abstract field of green worms and dots. West's works record the performative nature of her process. The actions she takes are implicit in creating the works and imbuing them with a physical, as well as organic, residue. West has stated, "Film is inherently alchemical, as it's made of layers of emulsion that are exposed to light or in my case, anything I want, that then produces 'gold' in the form of mesmerizing, colorful images."[22]

Erwin Wurm uses materials that embody characteristics of prior use, thereby becoming visual tools by which resemblance can be organized and identified.[23] The artist explains the origin of his use of everyday materials as a response to financial constraints when he was a student. He was forced to work with inexpensive materials, things discarded by other people, including clothing and even dust.[24] Wurm uses dust to record absence. It is a way of referencing both time and memory. As Walter Benjamin has observed, we see the new within the always-the-same and the always-the-same within the new. Wurm accomplishes this by suggesting a new reality when material is re-formed.[25]

Rudolf Stingel's *Untitled* (2002) [page 55], a shimmering, silver monochrome, is actually a large piece of Celotex insulation board. The imperfections scratched into the surface are the result of viewer interaction. Using coins, keys, pencils, or anything else that can be found, people leave the residue of their presence in the form of graffiti-like markings. Stingel complicates the Modernist form of large-scale monochromatic painting, trading paint on canvas for material that is significantly mundane and potentially even toxic. Stingel's material reveals its own history while simultaneously conveying the active role that we as viewers can play in transformation, physical as well as conscious.

The idea of transformation is at the heart of Wolfgang Laib's practice. Laib utilizes natural materials such as pollen, milk, and beeswax, removed from their natural environment, in order to illuminate their essence. He has said, "I think the better the art is . . . the more it really makes a change to something else."[26] In thinking about human progress, Laib eloquently stated, "From day to day or year to year it may have been the politicians who marched into another country or did this and that, but eventually it was culture which somehow brought mankind to somewhere else."[27]

Laib's *Milkstones* appear to be solid pieces of pure white marble. With quite careful viewing it is possible to notice that the surface is not static, but rather a finely balanced concavity created from milk poured to the exact point of suspension. When we realize that something is not as we previously thought it to be, the opportunity for transcendence occurs. This possibility—and its always-present counter, impossibility—sanctions the notion that art can, as Laib posits, positively change the world.

Felix Gonzalez-Torres works with objects just as they are: lightbulbs and plastic beads. He leaves the installation and even the sourcing of the materials to the exhibitor. The light strands evoke varied references—from safety to spirituality to impermanence—depending on how they are installed, either suspended from the ceiling or lying on the floor, indoors or outside, stretched out in a clean line or messily gathered. Gonzalez-Torres's works are inspired by everyday events, personal biography, and the challenges of late-twentieth-century life.[28] In an interview with Robert Nickas, the artist stated, "Meaning is created once something can be related to personal experience."[29]

Gonzalez-Torres creates works that necessitate viewer participation. By generously offering the viewer a role in the work, both in its perception and in the construction of its meaning, the experience becomes deeply personal.

Dieter Roth is also known for utilizing pedestrian materials, although often he employs elements prone to decomposition, questioning their nature and sustainability: cheese, chocolate, rabbit droppings, tar, glue, cocoa powder, sour milk, moldy foods, and licorice sticks, among them. By employing found objects, Roth facilitates the viewer's remembrance of their past use and function. The resulting insight into the choices of materials allows the viewer to align his or her perception with that of the artist.[30] Because the viewer recognizes what he or she is looking at materially, the perceptual acknowledgment of visual alchemy is resounding. Roth's is a mythic materiality.

Alexandra Bircken assembles natural elements, such as sticks and twigs, and wraps them with brightly colored yarn. Often suspended from the ceiling or attached to the wall, these orblike objects resemble tumors, growths, or other biomorphic disfigurations, camouflaged by aestheticized decoration.

Similar to Alexandra Bircken, Anna Sew Hoy employs and combines diverse materials in an idiosyncratic way. The focuses of her works are odd circular ceramic elements through and upon which other elements are added, threaded, or suspended. She utilizes chains and denim to create works that are simultaneously anthropomorphic—visually as well as with titles such as *Heart* (2007) [page 73] and *Two Eyes* (2007) [page 75]—and abstract. Each hangs on the wall supported by a single screw, evoking a Native American dream catcher, your car and house keys, or a character from an L. Frank Baum novel. As Hoy herself has commented, "I zoom in on the object and try to give it a new life, realize its potential to be transformed and to achieve new meaning or significance."[31]

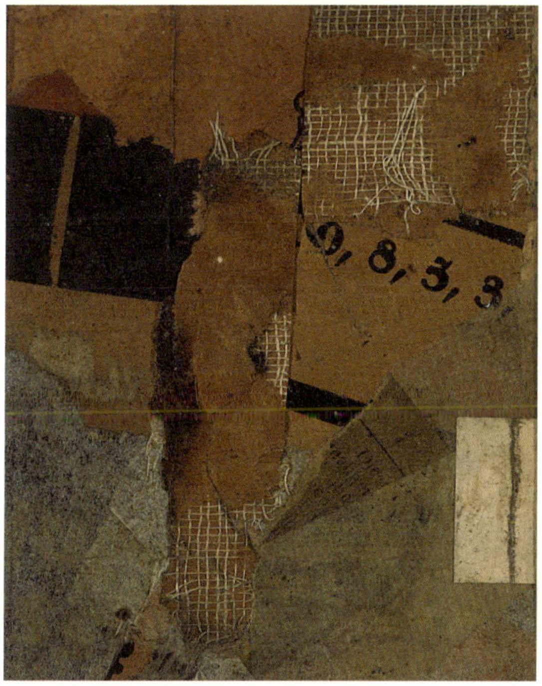

Kurt Schwitters, *Mz 129 rot oben [Mz 129 Red on top]*, 1920

Mitzi Pederson utilizes simple, raw materials and combines them in unexpected, enchanting ways. *Untitled* (2008) [page 77] bears an intriguing relationship to Friedman's *Two by Four*, as here Pederson also uses a piece of wood that is leaned against a wall. Pederson's wood is just that, though, with the subtle addition of silver leaf. Another untitled work, made of a cinder block, wood, sand, glue, and string, is intentionally modest in its materials, while mimicking classical modernist sculptural forms. Its charm lies in the small length of blue string that stretches across the vertical lengths. Its extension and connection are more like an elegant spider's web than a piece of structural support. Pederson transforms these utilitarian materials through the additive nature of collage. The items she uses are the things themselves but, together, become something altogether more.

The work that William O'Brien created specifically for *Now You See It* suggests a complex, insular world engulfed by a dark cover. A grouping of mildly figurative objects cowers together on a low, black table set against a cosmically oriented drawing. While the image could suggest a poetic nightscape, it also recalls the blindness, here black rather than white, of Saramago. Again the notion of rewarding a lingering view is evoked. One's engagement deepens beyond the initial seduction. Sometimes, when you stare at a work of art, you leave the place in which you have been and end up somewhere previously unimaginable.

There are many other artists who could have been included in this exhibition. Michael Asher used compressors in 1966–67 to create a series of works that consisted of columns or planes of accelerated air and which could be sited in a gallery or museum in reference to existing architectural elements. Developed out of the artist's questioning of standard viewer-object relationships, these works—which visitors would perceive only when walking through them—subtly altered and annotated existing pathways through an exhibition space.[32] Robert Barry's gas works utilized "invisibility as a means of evoking something immeasurable and without limit—the sublime realm of the unseen."[33] Seeing is often believing. We want to be shown evidence to verify truth. Barry plays into the possibilities inherent in knowledge that exclude seeing. As viewers, we must believe that Barry has done what he said he did. He introduces trust. Once inside the asylum, Saramago's characters, now blind, must trust in things that they also cannot see. The blindness necessitates turning to other means to navigate their existences. Vik Muniz defines art as a subtle connection between mind and matter. He re-creates iconic images while simultaneously revealing and debasing the process of their making.[34] Speaking during his abstract period, Philip Guston said, "The trouble with recognizable art is that it excludes too much." Guston is saying that what you see is what you see, and art provides the opportunity to communicate something more. If we are blind to our everyday life—due to its banality or repetition—art can facilitate a fissure, revealing something more, revealing vision itself. Asher, Barry, Muniz, and Guston are all engaging the process of celebrating the intangible, embracing the unknown, unseen, and unrecognizable as magical spaces equipped to celebrate the transformative qualities of art.

Conversely, Kurt Schwitters's assemblages made from scraps of refuse—what he termed "Merz"—have been called "Psychological Collage." These works were usually collages incorporating found objects and making humorous allusion to current events.[35] Without the influence of Schwitters, the work of O'Brien, Sibony, Pederson, and Hoy, among others, does not seem possible.

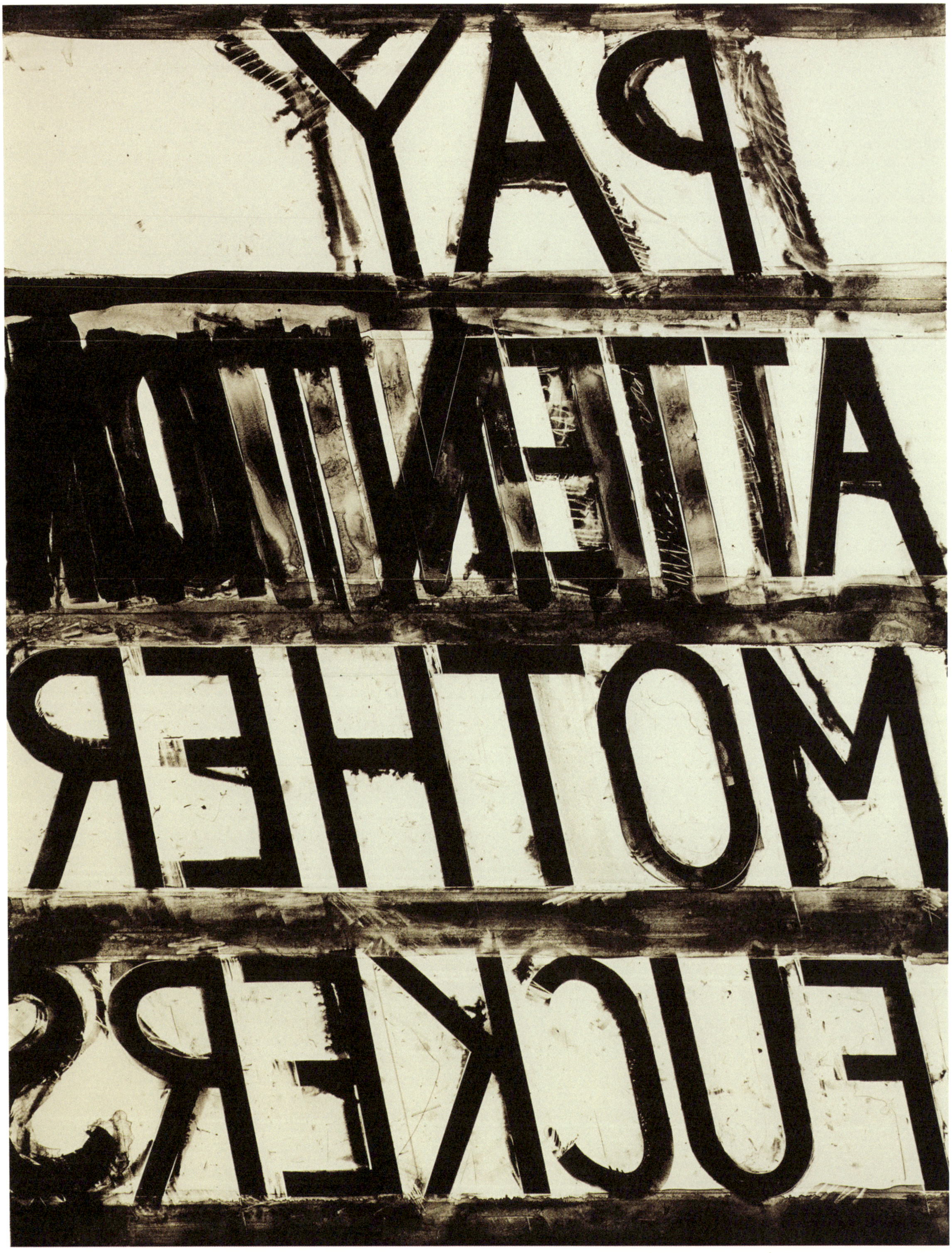

Bruce Nauman, *Pay Attention Mother Fuckers*, 1973

Seeing is intimately connected to our notions of truth, and in fact it underpins our belief in the world around us. As Rugoff noted, the bias toward the visual reached an apotheosis of sorts in the mid-1960s when Frank Stella formulated his famous "What you see is what you see" credo. One of the pioneers of Minimalism, Stella declared that in his paintings there was nothing "besides the paint on the canvas" and insisted that "only what can be seen there *is* there."[36] His perspective seems to come right out of Ryman's own insistences.

Describing the rationale of her work, Louise Bourgeois said in an interview with Paulo Herkenhoff, "It is all there because of the energy. Passing from one state to another, or the transformations."[37] She also recognizes, at the core of her work, "The resistance of the material corresponds to the insistence on coming to the core of the matter, it is an exact replica of the compulsion to understand."[38] Those efforts to see, know, be seen, and be known are a driving force for effort, interaction, and creation in art and in life.

Jasper Johns stated, "Do something, do something to that, and then do something to that." His efforts were directed at transformation of both need and notion. Within and among art we can find parameters for a better life. Bruce Nauman, in one of his first neon works from 1967, proclaims a private thought to the general public and utilizes a medium identified with commercial visual culture to make art that did not look like art: "The true artists helps the world by revealing mystic truths." Five years later, he created a limited-edition print that can be understood as a mantra for art that demands your awareness: "Pay Attention Mother Fuckers." But, if you, as the viewer, do not pay attention, what do you miss? Not only might you miss the subtle blues in a Reinhardt, the seemingly impossible balance in a Sibony, or the aura of a Friedman, you might in fact be blind to something greater, the ability to perceive beyond the here and now. Magic—whether in the sleight of hand of skilled magicians or the phenomenological play of visual artists—allows us to see it now. Once something is revealed (again) after it disappeared or was rendered invisible, the inherent value ascends. After the viewer stands in the space of unknowing, witnessing the aesthetic indeterminacy and seeking the embodied magic, what they may walk away knowing is that blindness is now an impossibility.

Heidi Zuckerman Jacobson is the Director and Chief Curator of the Aspen Art Museum.

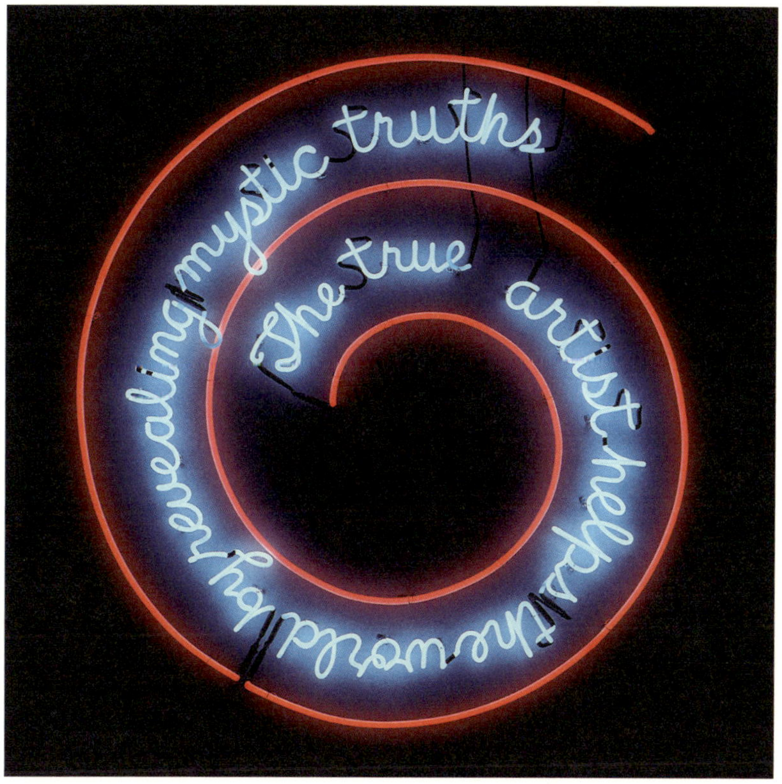

Bruce Nauman, *The True Artist Helps the World by Revealing Mystic Truths*, 1967

NOTES

1 John Newton, "Amazing Grace" (1779).
2 José Saramago, *Blindness* (CITY: PUBLISHER, YEAR), PAGE. [Complete citation TK.]
3 Ad Reinhardt quoted in Lucy Lippard, "Introduction to 557,087" in Conceptual Art: A Critical Anthology, ed. Alexander Alberro and Blake Stimson (Cambridge: MIT Press, 1999), 184.
4 *New York Times* art critic Holland Cotter wrote, "The primary reward [these paintings] offered was the experience of being with them, which, to be an experience . . . required patience and concentration in Holland Cotter, "Tall, Dark and Fragile," www.nytimes.com/2008/08/01/arts/design/01blac.html (accessed August 1, 2008).
5 Drake Bennett, "How magicians control your mind: Magic isn't just a bag of tricks—it's a finely-tuned technology for shaping what we see. How researchers are extracting its lessons," boston.com (accessed August 3, 2008).
6 Stephen L. Macknik, Mac King, James Randi, Apollo Robbins, Teller, John Thompson, and Susana Martinez-Conde, "Attention and awareness in stage magic: Turning tricks into research," *Nature Review Neuroscience* (published online July 30, 2008), 1.
7 Anthony Huberman, "I ♥ X Information," *Afterall*, 23.
8 Ralph Rugoff, *A Brief History of Invisible Art* (San Francisco: CCA Wattis Institute for Contemporary Arts, 2005), 17.
9 Eva Respini, "Wade Guyton," *Greater New York 2005* (Long Island City: P.S.1 Contemporary Art Center, 2005), 172.
10 Charles Wylie, *Robert Ryman* (New Haven and London: Yale University Press, 2006), 6.
11 Ibid., 10.
12 Ibid., 57.
13 "Gedi Sibony," *New Yorker*, May 26, 2008.
14 Sarah Hermanson Meister, "Gedi Sibony," *Greater New York 2005* (Long Island City: P.S.1 Contemporary Art Center, 2005), 314.
15 Gedi Sibony," *New Yorker*, May 26, 2008.
16 Claes Oldenburg, Andy Warhol, Robert Morris, and Benjamin H. D. Buchloh, "Three Conversations in 1985: Claes Oldenburg, Andy Warhol, Robert Morris," *Duchamp Effect*, October 70 (Autumn 1994): 64.
17 Ibid.
18 Lynne Cooke, "Lawrence Weiner Displacement," Dia Art Foundation, http://www.diaart.org.
19 Fred Sandback, "Remarks on My Sculpture," Dia Art Foundation, http://www.diachelsea.org.
20 Ibid., 37.
21 Ron Platt, *Tom Friedman* (Winston-Salem: Southeastern Center for Contemporary Art), 5.
22 Greg Kurcewicz, "Jennifer West Interview," www.kurcewicz.co.uk/ (accessed May 23, 2008).
23 Gary Dufour, "Replenishing a Void," in *Erwin Wurm* (Vienna: Wiener Secession, 1990), 33.
24 "Interview: Erwin Wurm," www.kopenhaden.dk (accessed June 26, 2008).
25 Gary Dufour, "Replenishing a Void," in *Erwin Wurm* (Vienna: Wiener Secession, 1990), 33.
26 Wolfgang Laib, *Journal of Contemporary Art*.
27 Darren James Jorgensen, "Wolfgang Laib: Retuning to What Is, an Interview with Wolfgang Laib," *e-maj* (July1–December 2005), 5.4.
28 Amanda Cruz, "The Means of Pleasure," in *Felix Gonzalez-Torres* (Los Angeles: The Museum of Contemporary Art, 1994), 22.
29 Ann Goldstein, "Untitled (Ravenswood)," in *Felix Gonzalez-Torres* (Los Angeles: The Museum of Contemporary Art, 1994), 41.
30 Craig Saper, "Review: Dieter Roth," *Art Journal 59*, no. 1 (Spring 2000): 108.
31 Asia Society, "one way or another: Asian American Art Show."
32 Ralph Rugoff, *A Brief History of Invisible Art* (San Francisco: CCA Wattis Institute for Contemporary Arts, 2005), 9.
33 Ibid., 11.
34 Vik Muniz: *verso*," Sikkema Jenkins & Co.
35 "Kurt Schwitters," http://en.wikipedia.org/wiki/Kurt_Schwitters.
36 Ralph Rugoff, *A Brief History of Invisible Art* (San Francisco: CCA Wattis Institute for Contemporary Arts, 2005), 8.
37 Francis Morris, ed., *Louise Bourgeois* (Tate Modern, London, and the Museum of Contemporary Art, Los Angeles), 174.
38 Ibid.

We live in an age marked by both a lack of secrecy and a sense that secrets abound. Whether the result of an overabundance of personal information volunteered into the digital realm, or unfettered governmental surveillance, privacy and confidence seem ever less important and harder to protect. In this climate, secrecy has had to find new places to hide, and perhaps counterintuitively, it has made its way into the most ordinary and obvious. In the election-frenzied intimations of anti-American tendencies concealed within the ranks of Congress, or in those unattended bags that could be bombs, conspiracy surrounds us, and even the most well-lit places can harbor shadows.

A similar paranoia suffused the heyday of Cold War America, and perhaps it is no surprise that a material interest in secrecy and hiding was common to American art of the late 1960s and early '70s. In 1969, for example, Douglas Huebler wrote to his students at Bradford Junior College in Massachusetts, asking them to join him in a special project. "I need to use an important secret of yours in order to complete a project on which I am working," he implored. "Simply write it down and then burn the paper on which it is written in an ashtray, seal the ashes in an envelope addressed to me and have it put into my faculty mail box. I will complete the project by combining all ashes so returned into one mixture and then scattering it randomly around campus."[1] Secrecy assumed physical form in a number of Bruce Nauman's works made during the late '60s, notably his *John Coltrane Piece* (1968), which conceals a mirror on the bottom of a steel plate, blindly reflecting only the floor upon which it sits. Nauman's title suggests the performative element of his attraction to the clandestine, and he was interested in Coltrane because the saxophonist periodically turned his back on the audience—rehearsing, on the stage of a jazz club, the essential dialectic of aesthetic philosophy, between inside and outside, between the visible and the hidden, and the desire we have for that which appears to be withheld from us.

Although secrecy was most evident in the work of artists who, like Huebler and Nauman, we associate with the development of Conceptual Art, concealment featured in one of the main critiques levied against Minimalism. The critic and art historian Michael Fried charged that the boxes of Donald Judd and Robert Morris are "hollow," protesting the way in which they draw our minds to their "having an *inside*."[2] A work of art is, in Fried's assessment, meant to exist completely on the level of the visible; the suggested interiority of Judd's and Morris's sculptures was criminal, like a concealed weapon, because we couldn't see it. He bemoaned the "hidden naturalism" of their work, evoking an epistemological battle between surface and depth (along with its

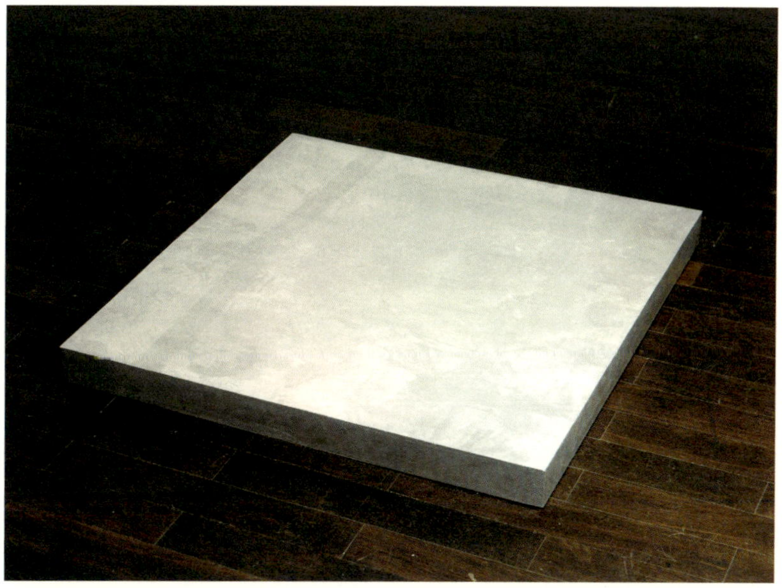

Bruce Nauman, *John Coltrane Piece*, 1968

contingent questions of subjective truth) that long predated both Coltrane and Minimalism.[3]

In the previous century, for example, naturalist fiction writers pursued the world at face value, while their realist counterparts sought to expose its underlying structures. The differences between the Impressionist painters and the Cubists and Constructivists who followed them can be arrayed along similar lines, and indeed, the early modernist manifestos often speak in the terms of veracity and authenticity. Kasimir Malevich described "a need for *truth*, not *sincerity*," and Georges Braque said that the purpose of painting is "not to *reconstitute* an anecdotal fact but to *constitute* a pictorial fact."[4] Malevich and Braque, like their realist forebears in literature, sought a penetrating kind of vision that displayed the bones of things, exposing their concealed essentiality. "The Realistic Manifesto" (1920) of Naum Gabo and Anton Pevsner emphatically connected interior structure with truth, describing the artist working as "the engineer constructs his bridges," in search of "the innermost essence of a thing."[5] For them, realism erased the aesthetic distinction between façades and what lies beneath them, simply divulging the world in full. "One cannot measure space in volumes as one cannot measure liquid in yards," they wrote. "Look at our space . . . what is it if not one continuous depth?"[6]

Morris insisted that he was continuing the formal indivisibility celebrated by Gabo, Pevsner, and their Constructivist peers, but Fried's assertion of the hidden interior of Minimalist sculpture conflicted with this notion of a "continuous depth."[7] In other words, you couldn't be hiding something and claim complete transparency.

For Fried, however, the greater sin of the "literalist sensibility" was less about what it might be hiding than what he considered to be its "theatricality." Theater, of course, includes an assumption of artifice, and thereby disguise—a stage actor may be said to be hiding behind the character, and conversely, an object that is hiding something is, in some way, acting. But Fried's critique had as much to do with theater's presumption of audience as with its artifice. He believed that art should exist timelessly on its own terms, without depending upon being seen, and he accused its practitioners of making objects that lie in wait for the viewer, like a kind of trap.

Clement Greenberg, interestingly, saw something similarly startling in the "desperation" of Conceptual Art, arising from a kind of deep boredom that he considered to be practically indifferent to its audience. "It's as though Conceptual Art says, all right, we are going to turn around on you, we are not going to give you any surprises at all, and there won't be an expectation involved either." In Greenberg's formulation, Conceptual Art, like Coltrane, turns its back on us, and in this rejection of audience the critic somewhat paradoxically found that the ensuing boredom can assume its own kind of theatricality. Still speaking in the voice of the conceptualist, he continued that "you are going to get boredom so undifferentiated as to constitute a surprise all in itself. This solid, monolithic, unadulterated, undifferentiated boredom will really stand you off and be our memorial."[8] Minimal and Conceptual strategies seem to be continually reasserting themselves in recent art, but Fried and Greenberg, taken together, suggest that these two strands running out of the 1960s might be best considered on a kind of performative continuum that is rooted, on some level, in a shallow game of secrecy and revelation. Somewhere between the dumb theatricality of Minimalism and the theatrical dumbness of Conceptual Art lays an entire swath of contemporary art, if not the sensibility of a generation.

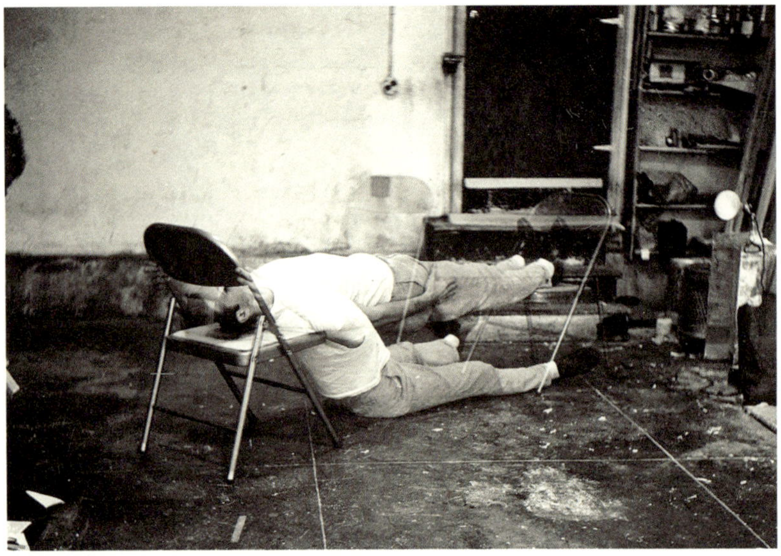

Bruce Nauman, *Failure to Levitate in the Studio*, 1966

The notion of a dumb kind of theatricality and its connection to hidden truth is most easily traced not to art criticism but to theater itself, where the Polish director and theorist Jerzy Grotowski had coined the term "poor theater" two years prior to Fried's seminal 1967 article. In contrast to nineteenth-century conceptions of naturalist acting, in which the actor disappeared behind the character, Grotowski described a stripped-down approach to performance that emphasized a kind of purity, what he termed "the discarding of masks, the revealing of the real substance."[9] Far from putting on airs, his theater was one of disclosure, of confession, in which the primary transformation occurring during a performance was one that exposed the actor most essentially.

A similarly demonstrative poverty is abundant in current art, and Gedi Sibony is one of its preeminent masters, arriving from Minimalism's literalist sensibility but subtly altering its melodrama. Sibony appears to celebrate what Greenberg called "the look of non-art," except that the artist's arrangements of cardboard, industrial carpet, tree branches, and other such prosaic materials lack any sense of high-minded rebellion or debasement [page #29]. At its best, Sibony's theatricality almost lacks risk, seeming too honest to fail, and yet perhaps not sincere enough to succeed. The Fluxus artist and publisher Dick Higgins saw the flirtation with failure as an essential ingredient in good art, noting that "in order to build intellectual excitement into work there must always be the sense that it was a near miss—a near failure."[10] This is what he termed the requisite "danger" of art, and it is something Nauman internalized when he made his multiple-exposure photograph *Failing to Levitate in the Studio* (1966), in which we see the artist lying pathetically between two chairs in his studio, his theatrical levitation superimposed upon its inevitable failure. Sibony's power, notably, derives similarly from disappointment, but with a different sequence of effort. The levitation in his work comes at the end, instead of first; the general state of his work begins in failure and abandonment rather than arriving there after much effort. Utterly lacking in danger, Sibony's slapstick shamanism elevates his materials practically by luck rather than will, rescuing them only briefly before returning them to their enduring condition of simple trash. His literalism is a kind of double negative, miming the feel of art borrowing the look of nonart, but ending up almost entirely recouped by its secular tedium once and for all. Rather than dress up, his art strips down, staying on the stage but donning only a ghostly costume. This should not be mistaken for laziness—if there is radicality in his art, it derives from his suggestion that the high drama of realism's revelation is rather lacking in drama after all. Now you see it, but it was here all along.

The mundane is valorized differently in the work of Ceal Floyer, who often uses unremarkable phenomena as material. As such, she is concerned less with what something is than how it behaves, which is one of the marks of the theatrical dumbness of the conceptual legacy that distinguishes it from simply poor theater. While Sibony begins and ends with the blandness of his vernacular supplies, the stuff of Floyer's art lies in the *performance* of that ordinariness, not in the materials themselves. She works with what we know and when we know it, and in this sense her art may be less about how the banal behaves than how we behave in the face of its factual stoicism. Rather than unveiling an effect, she belabors how it exists in the first place, and her epistemology, pointedly, is rooted in the *time* it takes to see these things for what they are, more than their actuality. Now you see it, sure, but how long has it been here?

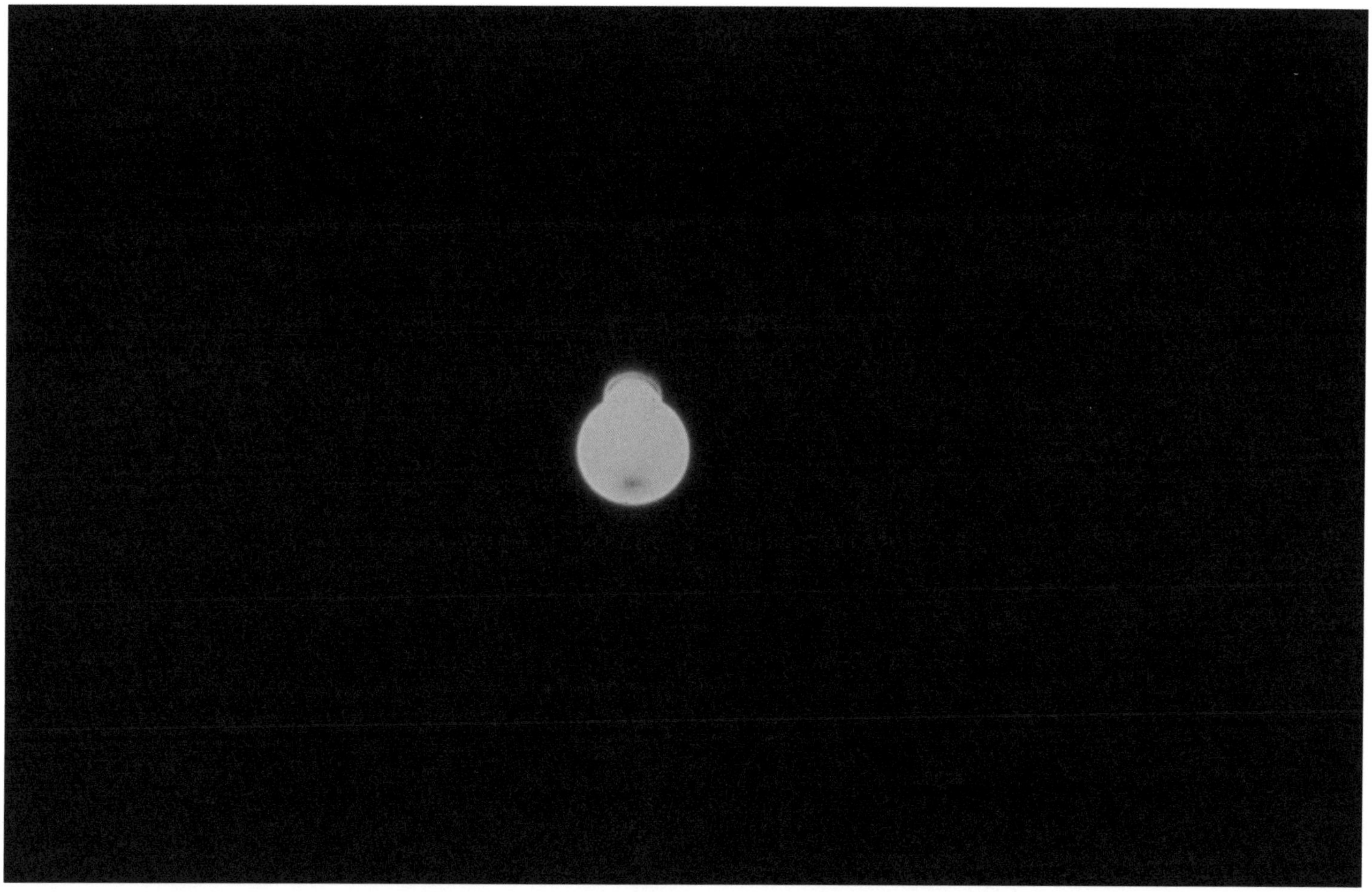

Ceal Floyer, *Light*, 1994 (installation view)

Like a bad magician, Floyer often uses absurdly inefficient kinds of formal trickery to flesh out this temporality. A lightbulb turns out to be illuminated from without, brightened by four spotlights in the corners of the room that are trained upon it. The sound of water dripping into a bucket is just that—a sound, emanating from a speaker sitting rather obviously in the bucket, its audio cable in plain view. The sliver of light under the bottom of a door, suggesting a lit room beyond the gallery, is a simple illusion, made by nothing more than a masked slide in a projector on the floor next to us [page 39]. In all of these cases, the brain trips over itself, kicking us because there is no sleight of hand, no real trick, and yet the setups are just too dumb for us to have paid them any notice initially. The burdensome physicality of her constructions conflicts with the quick elegance of their effect, and this makes for a frustrating kind of déjà vu, in which we feel as if we knew what is going on before we came to know it. With an embarrassing overliterality, Floyer creates little traps that give rise to the indifferent surprise Greenberg found in Conceptual Art, though we begrudge them that power. If Sibony's work displays "continuous depth," Floyer can be said to move in the other direction, adding a transparent extra layer onto the surface of the world. This layer magnifies its mundane substrate, creating an excess of knowledge, a kind of supernatural realism.

That excess of knowledge has its own limits, however, and we find it in Tom Friedman's *1,000 Hours of Staring* (1992–97) [page 43], which seems both excessive and miserly in equal parts. Friedman's bare sheet of paper doesn't even flirt with the nihilist air of nonart, as Robert Rauschenberg did when he famously erased Willem de Kooning's drawing in 1953. And though totally blank, *1,000 Hours* is not at all about what is missing, erased, or denied, but rather oddly about what we can see. Radically without depth and yet completely continuous, the blinding light of its self-evidence would seem to deter a deeper looking, presenting itself as a final resolution of formal aesthetic empiricism.

Robert Rauschenberg, *Erased de Kooning Drawing*, 1953

Friedman, though, has gone it one better. There is no material theater in this work: the paper is just what it is. And there is no temporal performance, either, because there is nothing for us to discover. Time is monolithically part of Friedman's material, but without a way to measure it, we wonder if he is lying about how long he stared at this thing. In this sense, Friedman has made what Kirk Varnedoe might have considered the most complete "picture of nothing," what he described as "vessels of intelligence that appear utterly dumb," but with a new twist—call it the "suspiciously dumb," which, unlike the invisibility of some classic conceptualism, plays out entirely on the level of the visible.[11] His triumph, then, is to inject doubt into the obvious, and with it, judgment and thereby ethics—a politics of vision, in short.

And so what do we think we see? *1,000 Hours* simply refers, of course, to that duration of the artist's gaze, recorded immutably on the page, and the date of the work tells us the five years during which the staring was done. But what of the hours of everyone else since then who has seen it and tried to discern something, anything, in its blankness, including those of us now standing before it? Do these supplemental minutes of attention alter the work? Once aware of this problem, we find that we are looking at looking in the dumbest way possible without a mirror—a deep twist on Heisenberg's now-outdated principle of uncertainty, in which the location of subatomic particles are assumed to be influenced by our efforts to see them. Only in this case, the paradox is more basic, and more vertiginous: that which oscillates, like a hallucination, between the visible and invisible is nothing short of vision itself, and its ability to affect things in the world.

John Cage, in his legendary lecture on nothing of 1950, said, "I am here, and there is nothing to say. . . . What we require is silence; but what silence requires is that I go on talking."[12] When Cage finally gave us silence, two years later, composing a work for piano in which the performer sits tacitly before the instrument for four minutes and thirty-three seconds, he asked that we listen harder. Yet in drawing our attention to the ambient sounds around us—people coughing, shifting in their seats; a bird outside—he suggested that silence cannot be achieved, that even if he stopped talking, noise is still there. Expecting to find silence in the soundproof environment of an anechoic chamber, he was surprised to discover that even there, he heard the low sound of his blood pumping and the high tone of his nervous system humming. Varnedoe believed that our culture demands pictures of nothing in part because their blankness gives form to the sense of loss that has accompanied the progress of modernity. But what nothing demands, of course, is that we keep on looking, and pictures of nothing, then, can't really exist—if only because in looking, something is always seen.

Our response to terminal blandness reveals the impossibility of nothingness. Higgins, who was a student of Cage, believed that "boredom played a comparable role, in relation to intensity, that silence plays with sound, where each one heightens the other and frames it."[13] In other words, nothingness (the lack) and ennui (how we feel about it) became tools to be used against each other, enacting a kind of self-inoculation. What at first blush may seem to be the disappointment we experience in boredom turns out, as least initially, to be restorative. In the self-reflexive loop of *1,000 Hours'* content and form, no longer distinguishable from each other, something nevertheless accumulates, and Friedman's point is that the very act of looking—even at nothing—eventually leaves its own trace, like an invisible version of the burnish that graces the bronze toes of public statues. The spectral residue of vision is this work's true material, both obvious and secret, protected by the impossibility of being observed. To find proof of its existence, we need look no further than modern advertising, an economy of attention denoted by "impressions" that estimate the number of times something may be viewed.

But lost in all of this is the attention we give to that which cannot be seen, and the desire we have for the unknown and inaccessible, which never goes away. What, after all, could be more boring than a world without secrets? Nauman's face-down mirror and Huebler's burned confessions arose from an awareness of this platitude. As such, they are not about seeing at all, but rather about envisioning—about imagination, and the seductive fogginess of those places we cannot reach, the things we cannot know. They hew to the classical realist notion of truth, and they bolster its power and allure by keeping it hidden. You never see it, and that is precisely what ensures that it stays true.

The suspiciously dumb rejects the very existence of deeper truth in favor of some sincere faith, but it pointedly still embraces some notion of secrecy. The secret of *1,000 Hours* is contained in its title, and this suggestion of a covert history invites us to confuse an imaginary otherness into the plain banality of its blankness. What may be most remarkable about Friedman's sheet of paper, perhaps, is that it performs this politic so efficiently, marrying the reductive clarity of seeing with the untethered vagaries of imagination in almost perfect coincidence, to a degree possible otherwise only in complete darkness. This perverse equanimity—in which light is dark, dark is light; in which reality must be taken on faith, and the imaginary so easily assumes the habit of truth—may stand as a modest monument to our time.

But looking back from here, we can also see that *1,000 Hours* prophesied a new aesthetic of paranoia, one born of a lack of secrecy and yet molded under its threat. Cage outlined a particularly reductive theatricality, removing the subject from the stage in the hope that nothing, completely unveiled, would perform itself. Its legacy, however, exposes more about its audience, and what, in a kind of delusional auto-performance, we insinuate into its void. When all is revealed, we will still hide things, albeit in plain sight, because we need to. For some time now, it has no longer been a question of whether you may see something tinged with secrecy, but when and where, and then whether or not to say something.

Peter Eleey is Curator at the Walker Art Center.

Notes

[1] This text is part of Huebler's resulting work *Location Piece #8, Bradford, Massachusetts* (1969).
[2] Michael Fried, "Art and Objecthood," *Artforum 5* (Summer 1967): 19.
[3] Ibid.
[4] Kasimir Malevich, "From Cubism and Futurism to Suprematism: The New Realism in Painting," in *Art in Theory 1900–2000*, ed. Charles Harrison and Paul Wood (Malden, MA: Blackwell Publishing, 2003), 174; George Braque, "Thoughts on Painting," in ibid., 214.
[5] Naum Gabo and Anton Pevsner, "The Realistic Manifesto," in ibid., 299–300.
[6] Gabo and Pevsner, "Realistic Manifesto," 300.
[7] Furthermore, Fried noted that despite Morris's interest in the Constructivists, he and Judd opposed sculpture constructed "part by part," like that of David Smith or Anthony Caro. Fried, "Art and Objecthood," 12.
[8] Clement Greenberg, *Homemade Esthetics* (New York: Oxford University Press, 1999), 175–76.
[9] Jerzy Grotowski, "Statement of Principles," in *The Twentieth-Century Performance Reader*, ed. Michael Huxley and Noel Witts (London: Routledge, 2002), 217. On realism and naturalism in nineteenth-century acting, see, for example, Robert Gordon, *The Purpose of Playing: Modern Acting Theories in Perspective* (Ann Arbor: University of Michigan Press, 2006), 8–12.
[10] Dick Higgins, "Boredom and Danger" (1966) In Ina Blom, *Dick Higgins*, exh. cat. (Høvikodden, Norway: Henie Onstad Kunstsenter, 1995), 112.
[11] Kirk Varnedoe, *Pictures of Nothing* (Princeton: Princeton University Press, 2006), 271.
[12] John Cage, "Lecture on Silence," in *Silence* (Cambridge: MIT Press, 1966), 109.
[13] Higgins, "Boredom and Danger," 107.

Wade Guyton, *Untitled*, 2007

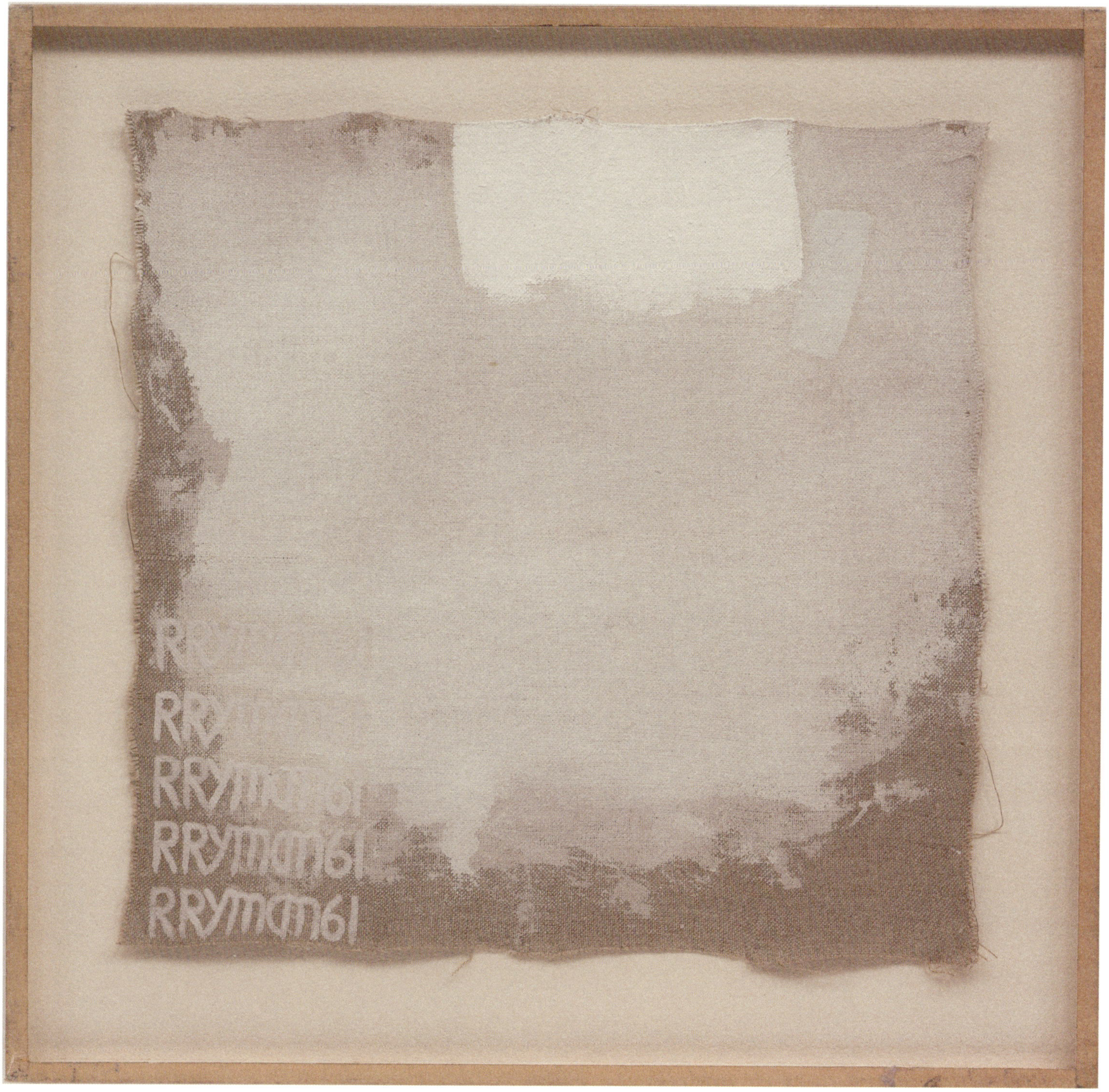

Robert Ryman, *Untitled,* 1961

Robert Ryman, *Series #22 (White)*, 2004

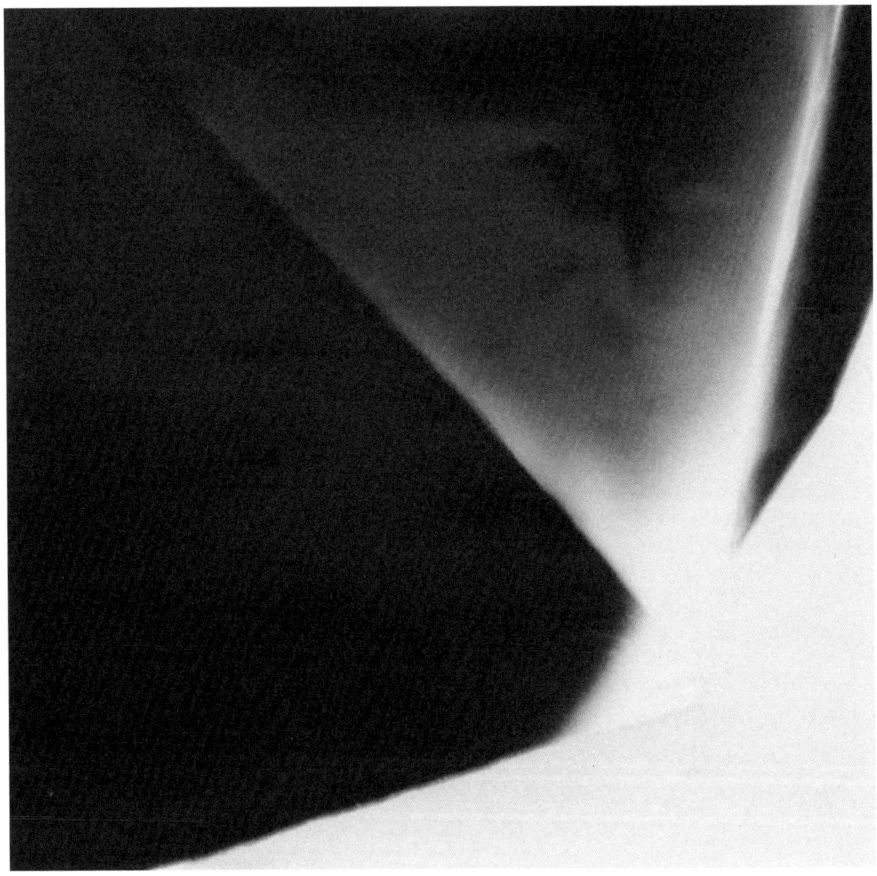

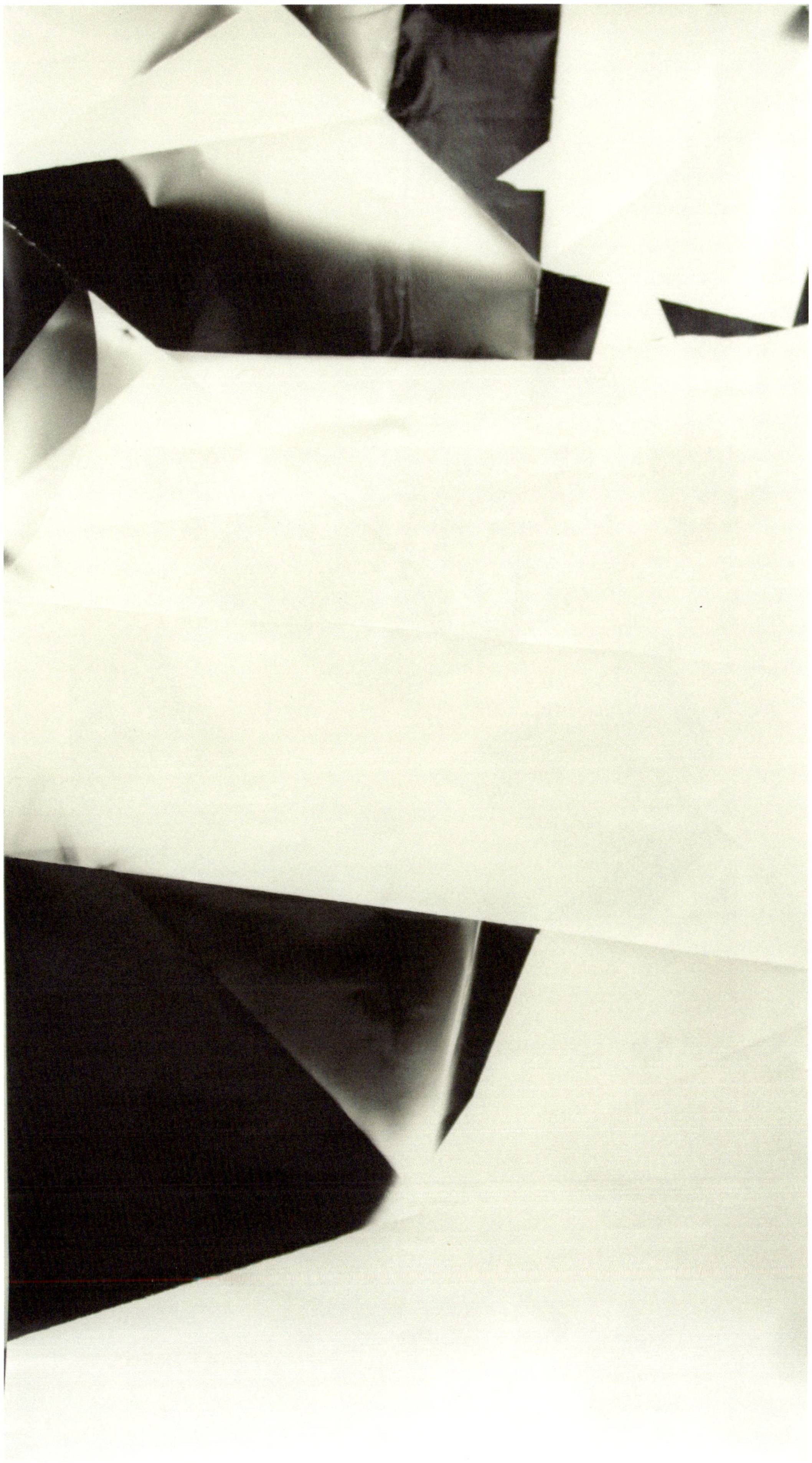

Walead Beshty, *Fold (Three Directional Light Sources, 35/62.5/145 degrees), December 22nd, 2006, Valencia, CA, Ilford Multigrade Fiber IV*, 2007

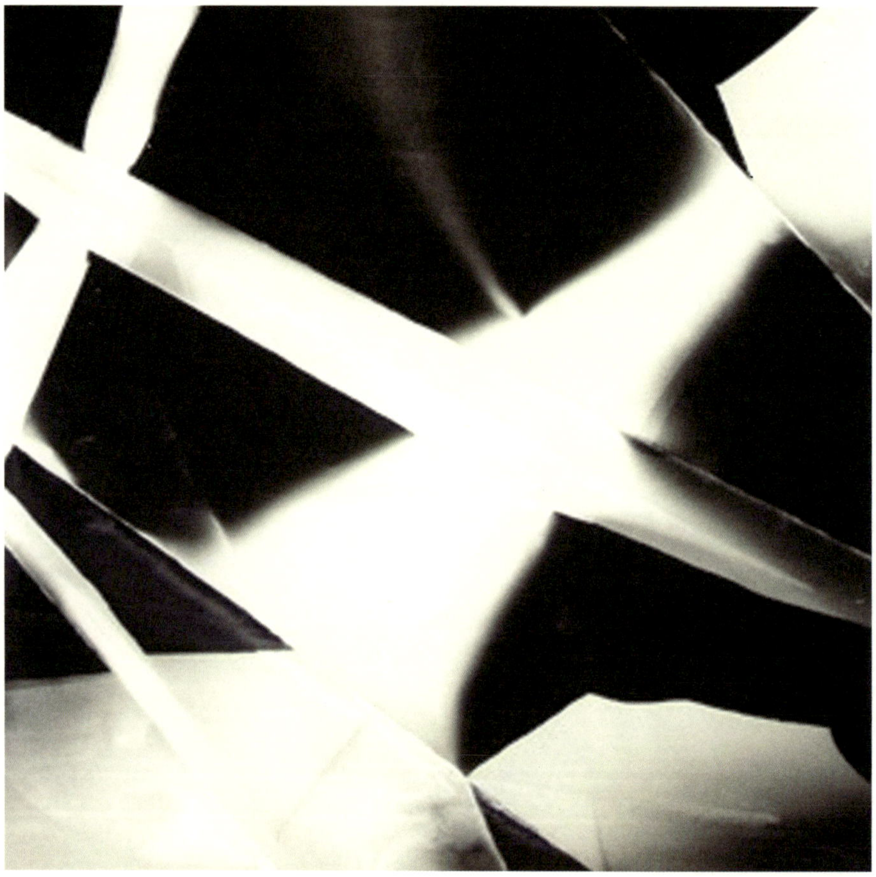

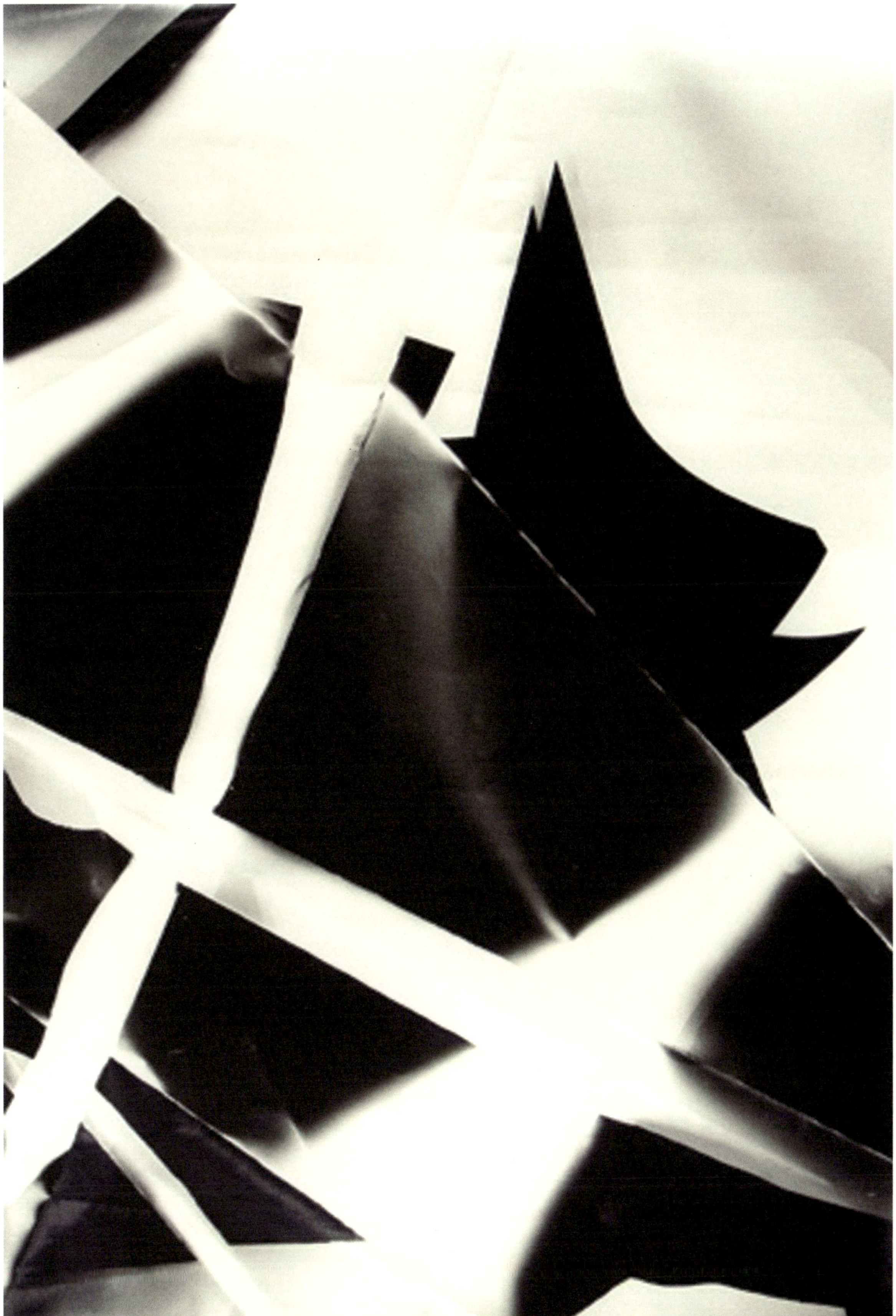

Walead Beshty, *Fold (80 degree directional light source) November 27th, 2006, Valencia, CA, Ilford, Multigrade fiber IV*, 2007

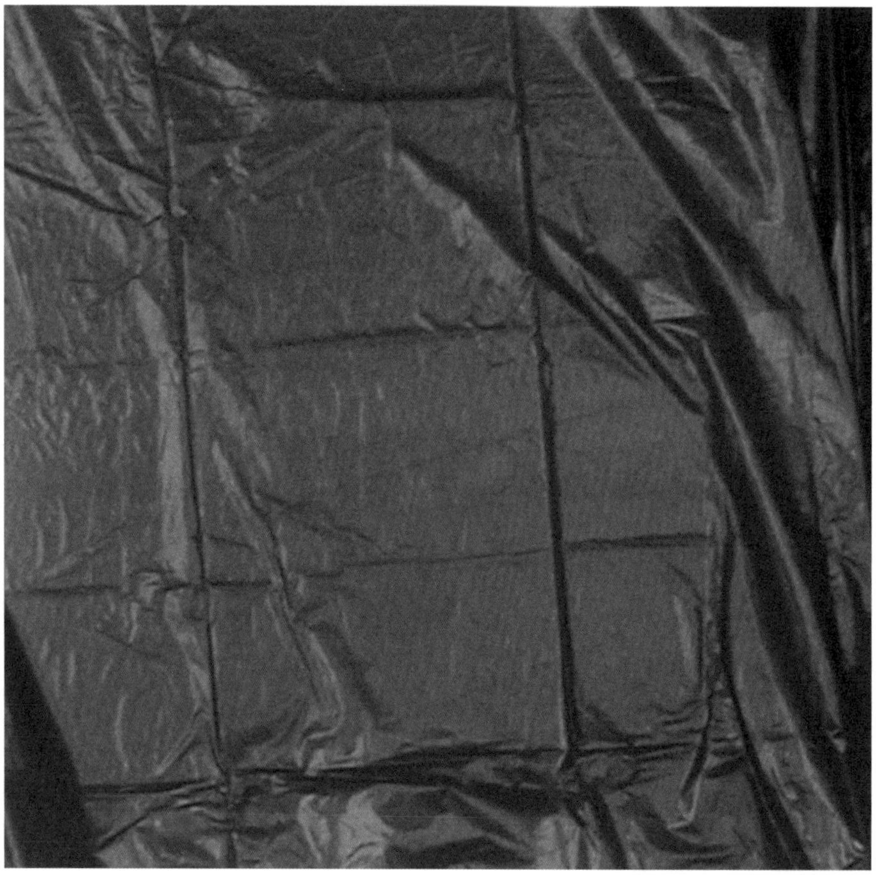

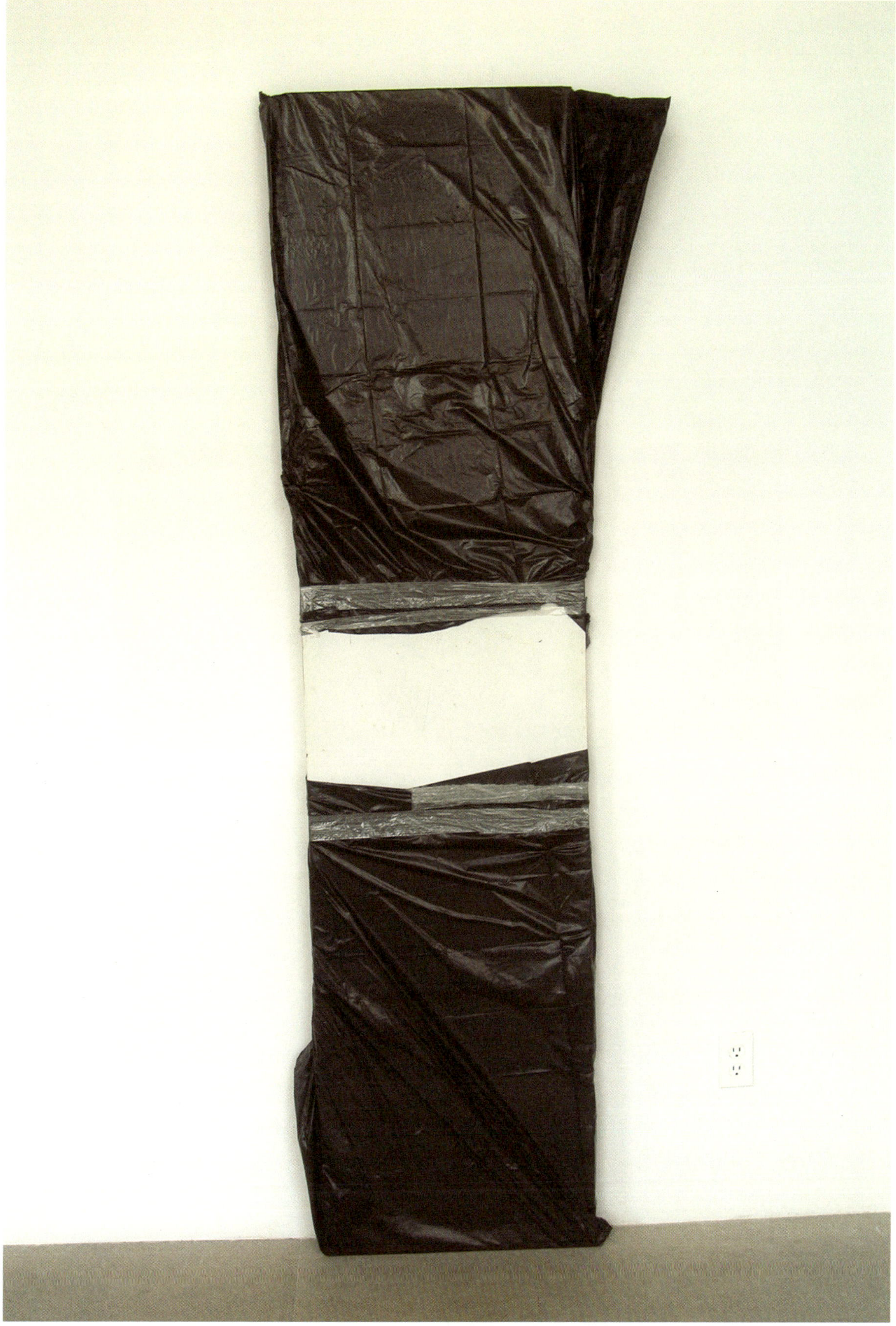

Gedi Sibony, *The Last One*, 2008

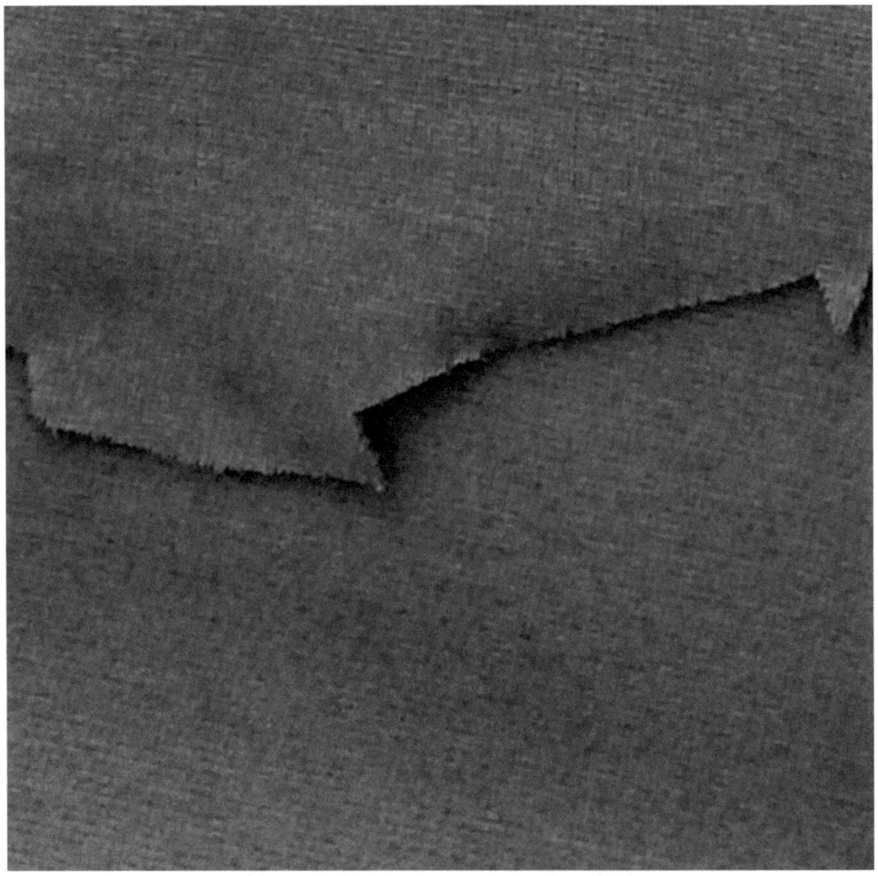

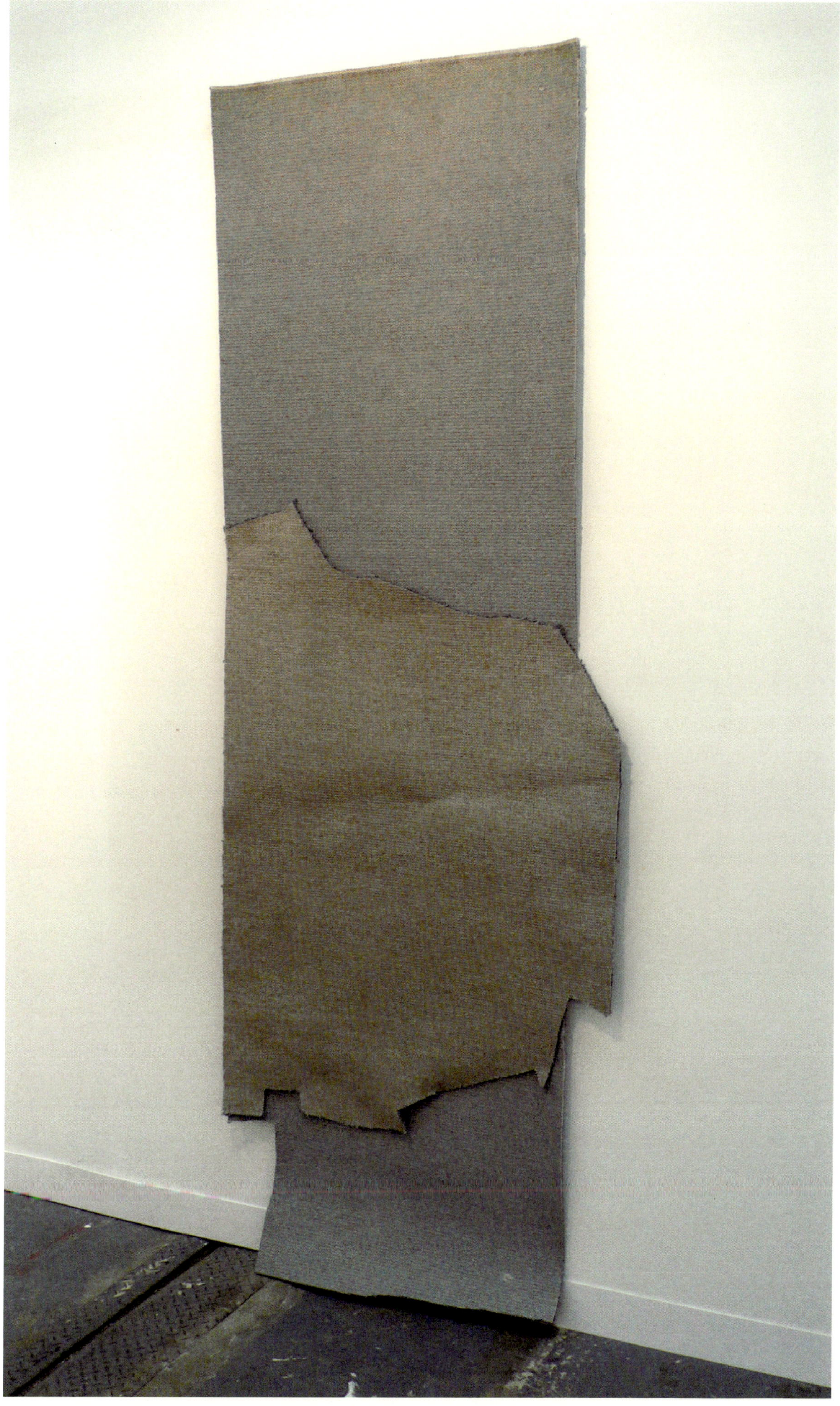

Gedi Sibony, *Left So Soon*, 2008

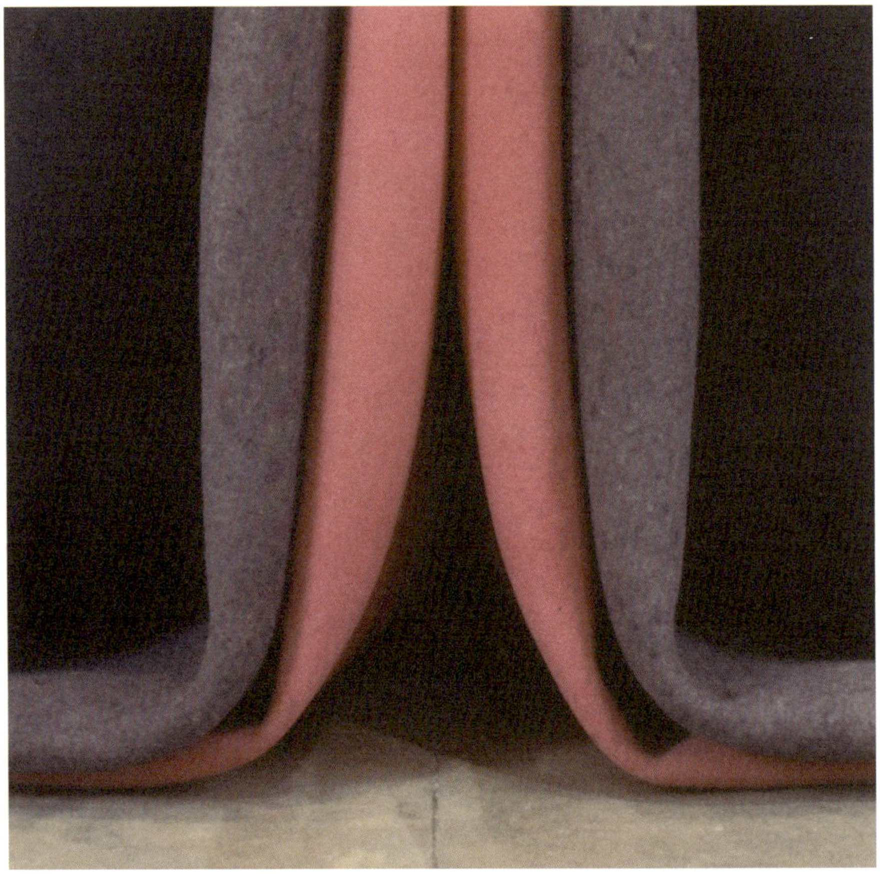

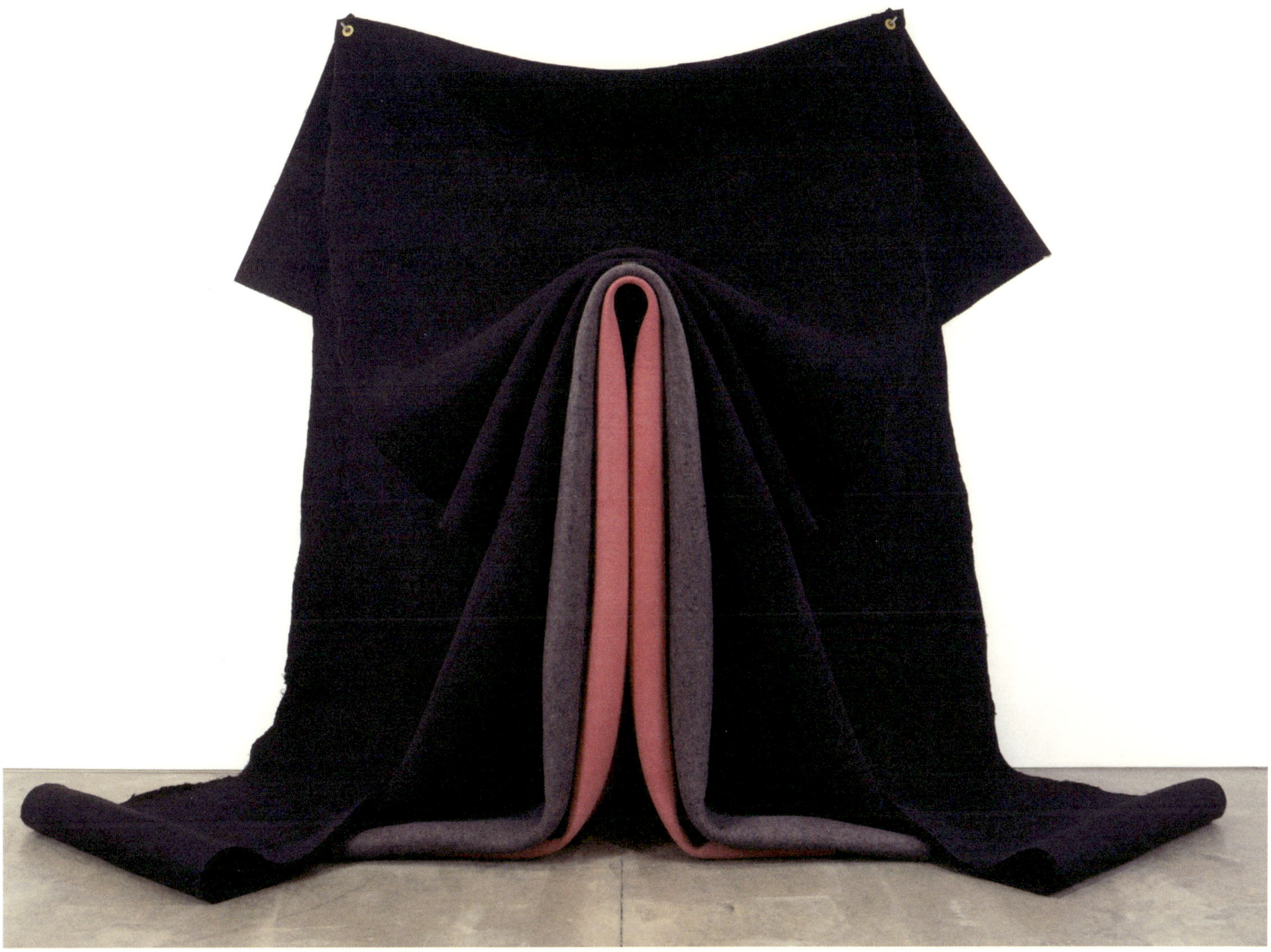

Robert Morris, *Vetti V*, 1993

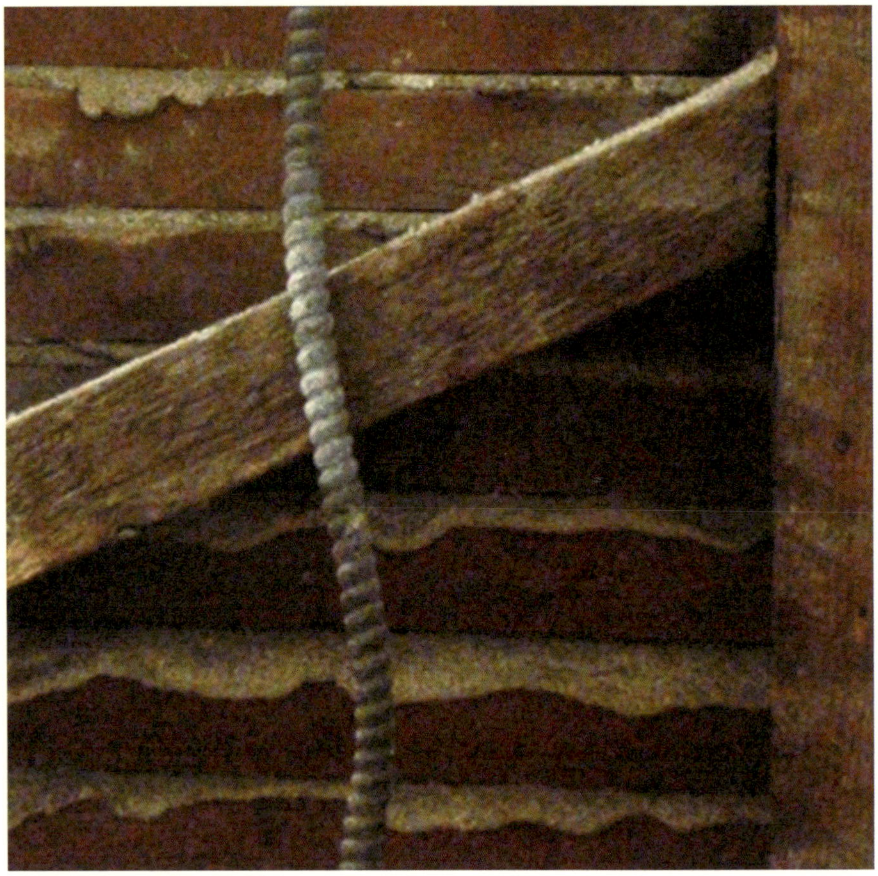

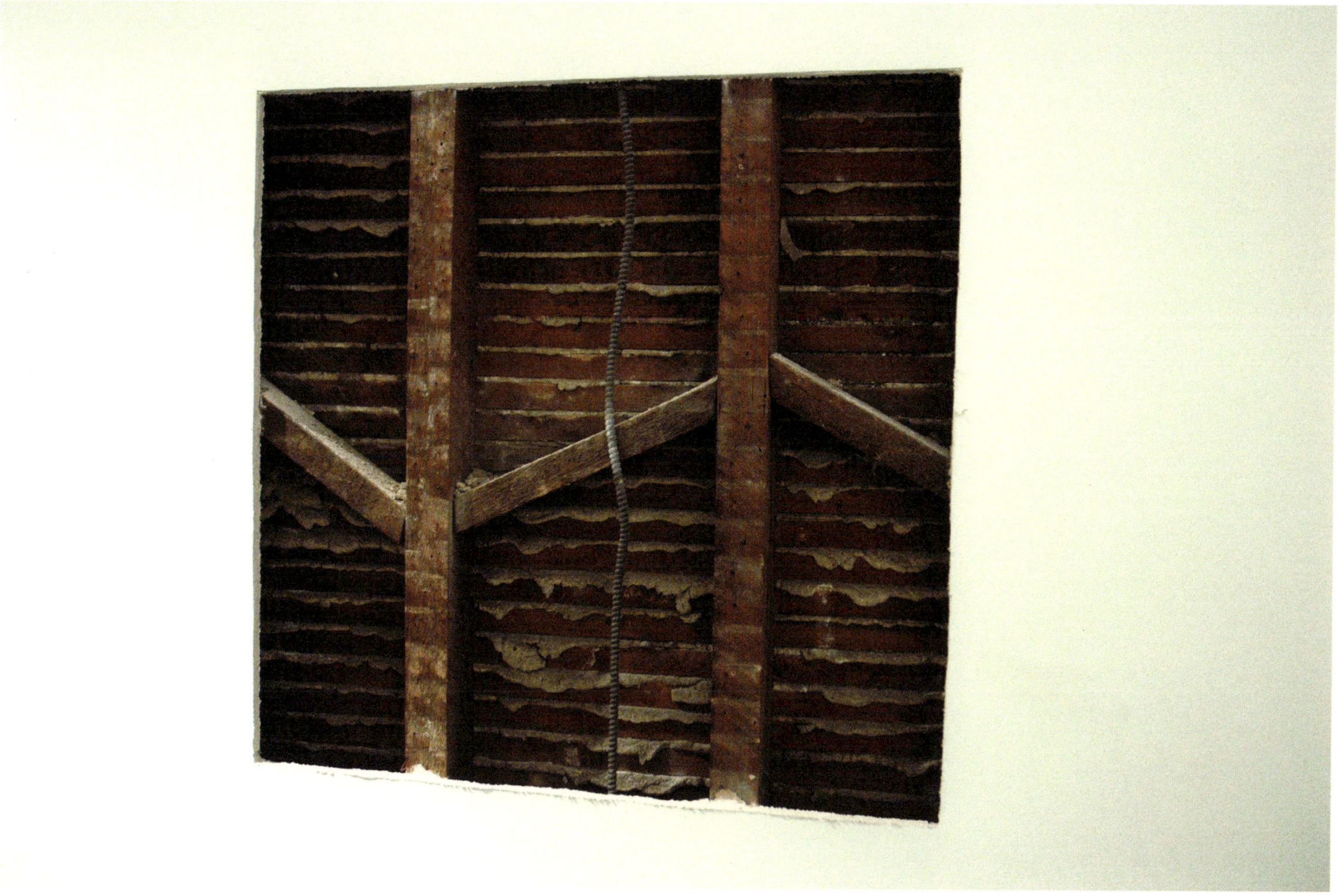

Lawrence Weiner, *A 36" X 36" REMOVAL TO THE LATHING OR SUPPORT WALL OF PLASTER OR WALLBOARD FROM A WALL*, 1968

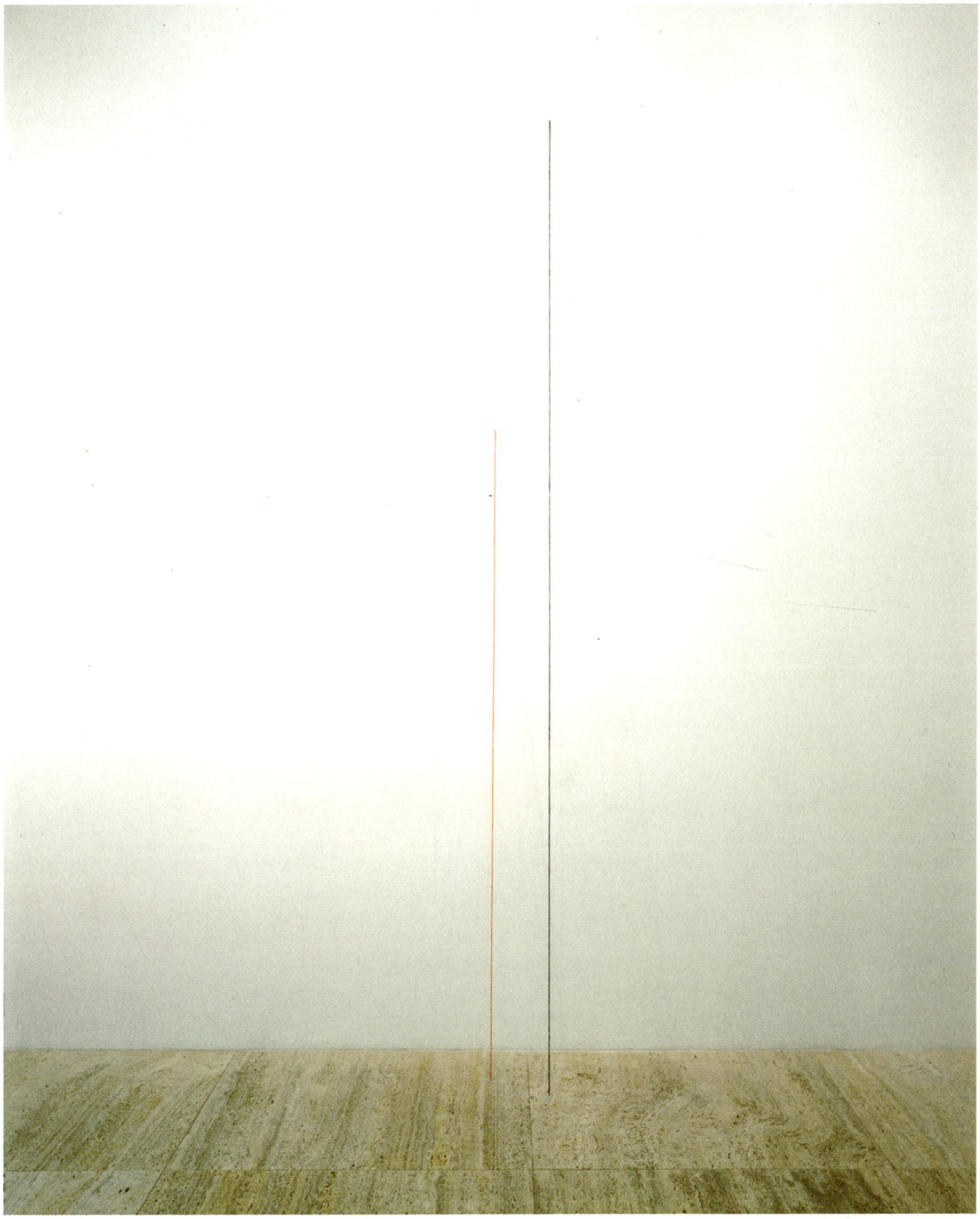

Fred Sandback, *Untitled (Sculptural Study, Two-part Leaning Construction)*, 1977/2004

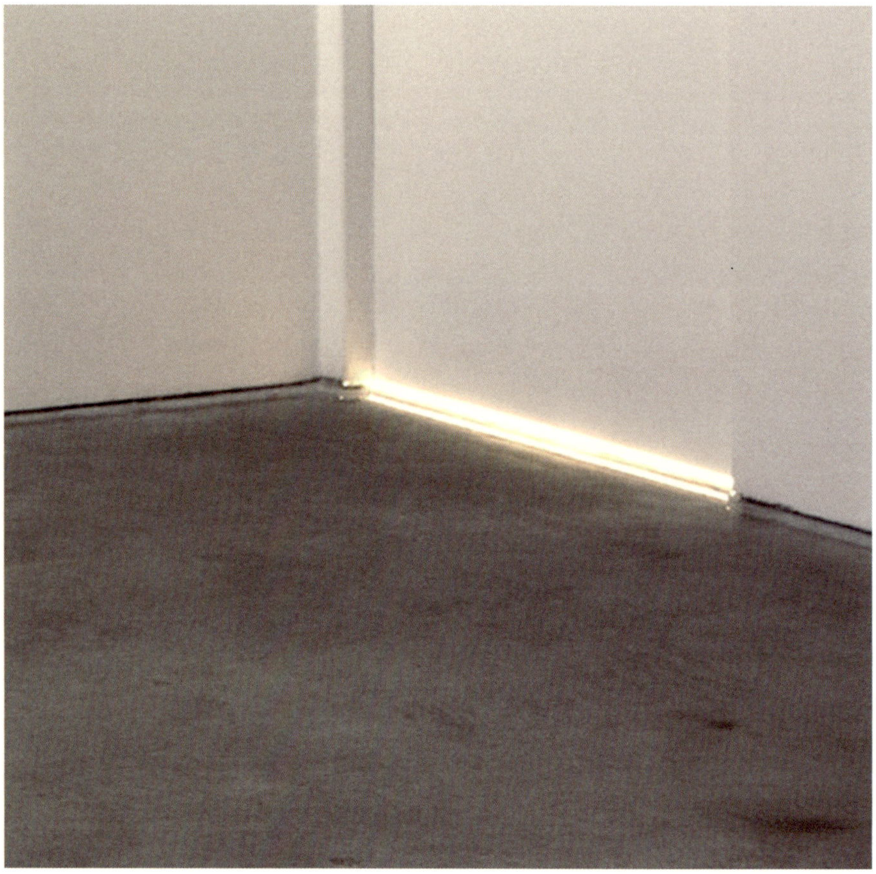

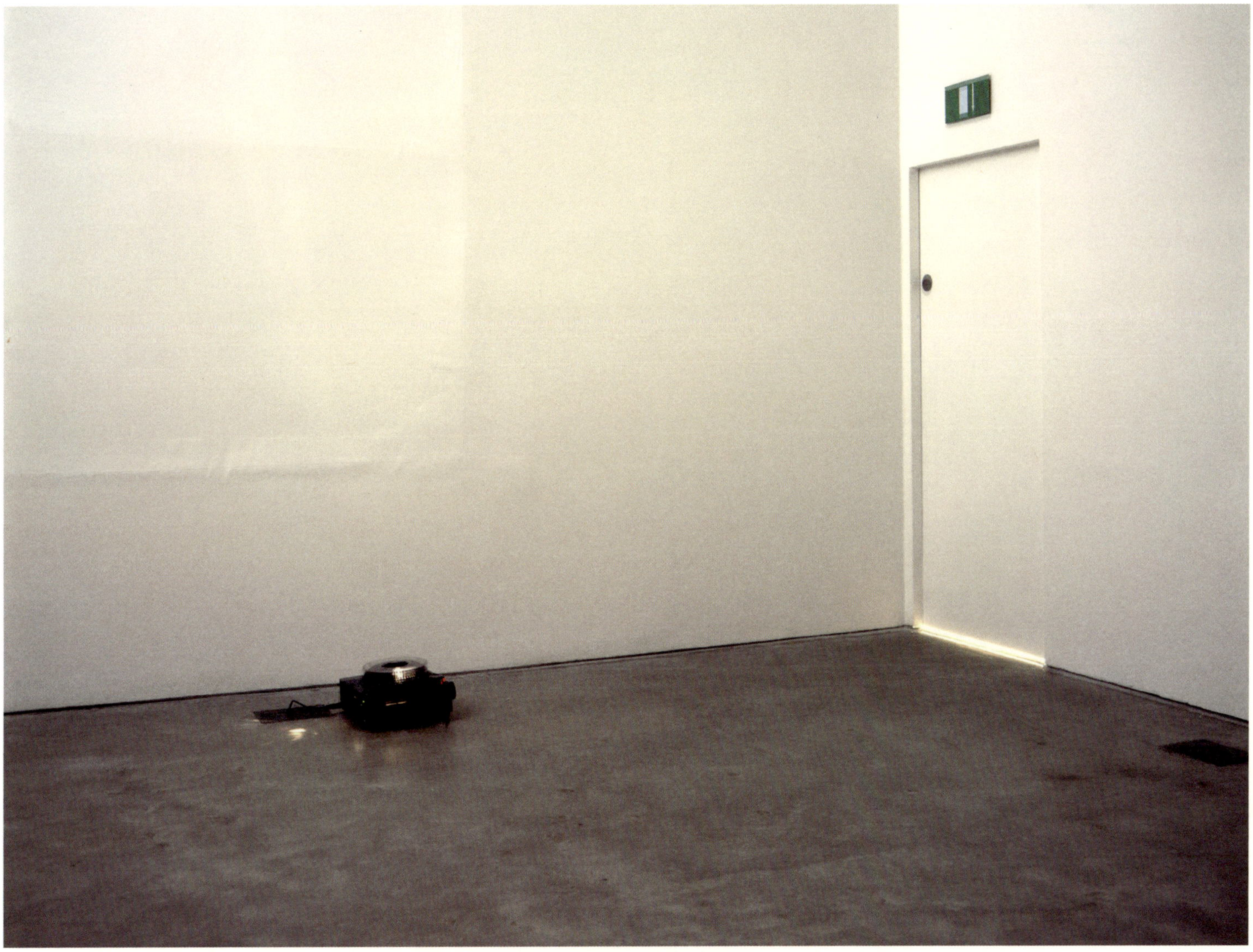

Ceal Floyer, *Door*, 1999

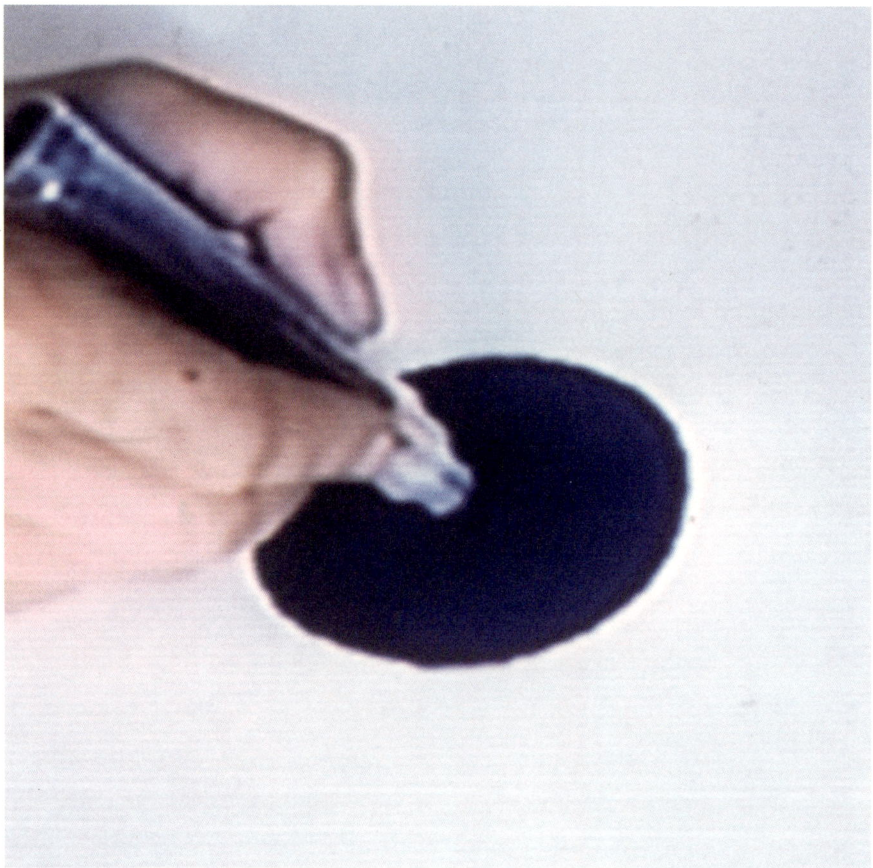

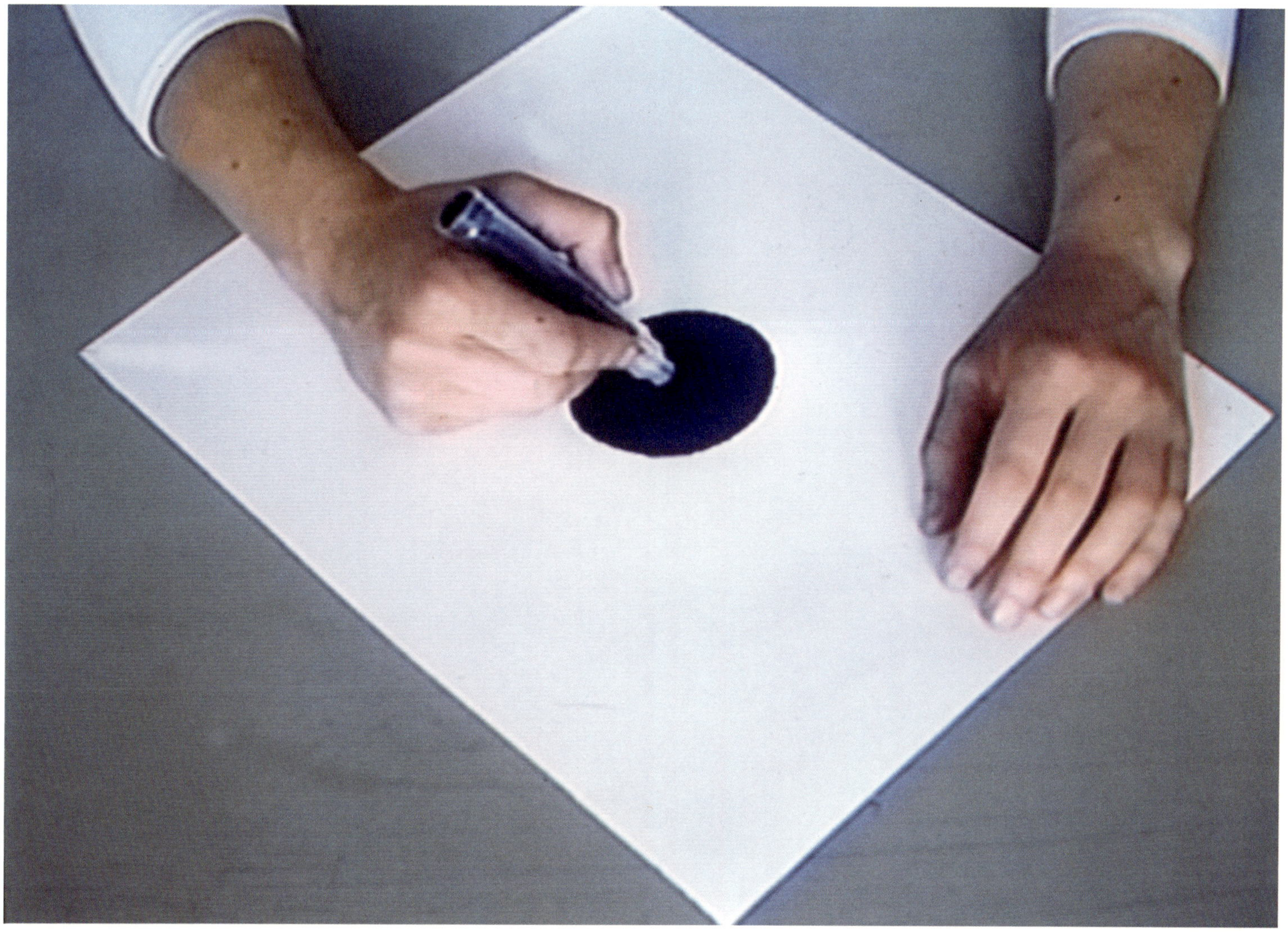

Ceal Floyer, *Ink on Paper (video)*, 1999

Tom Friedman, *1,000 Hours of Staring*, 1997

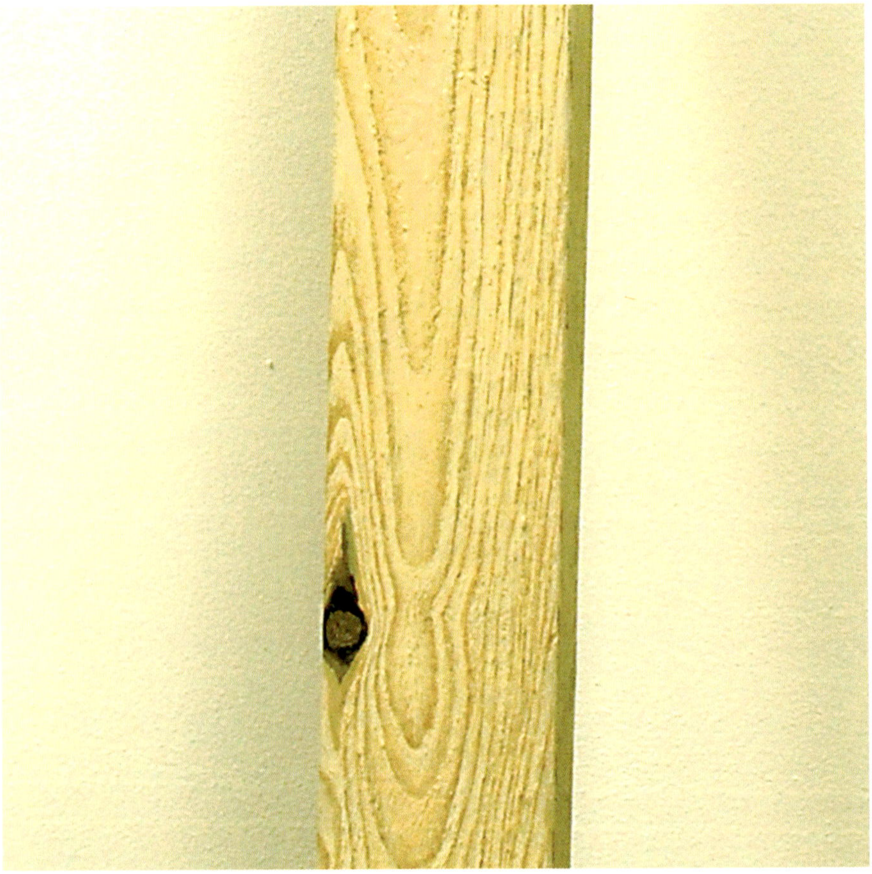

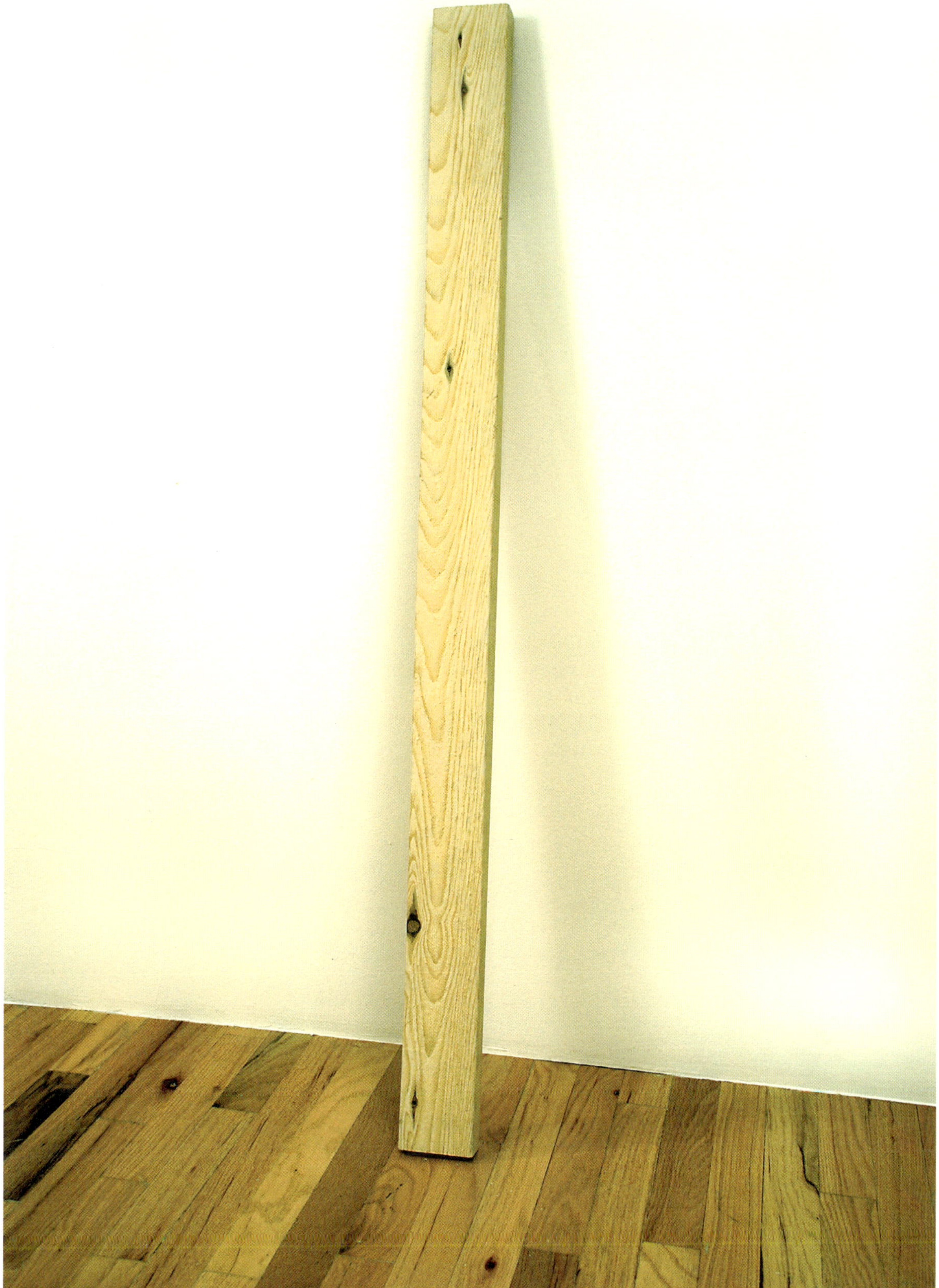

Tom Friedman, *Two by Four*, 1990

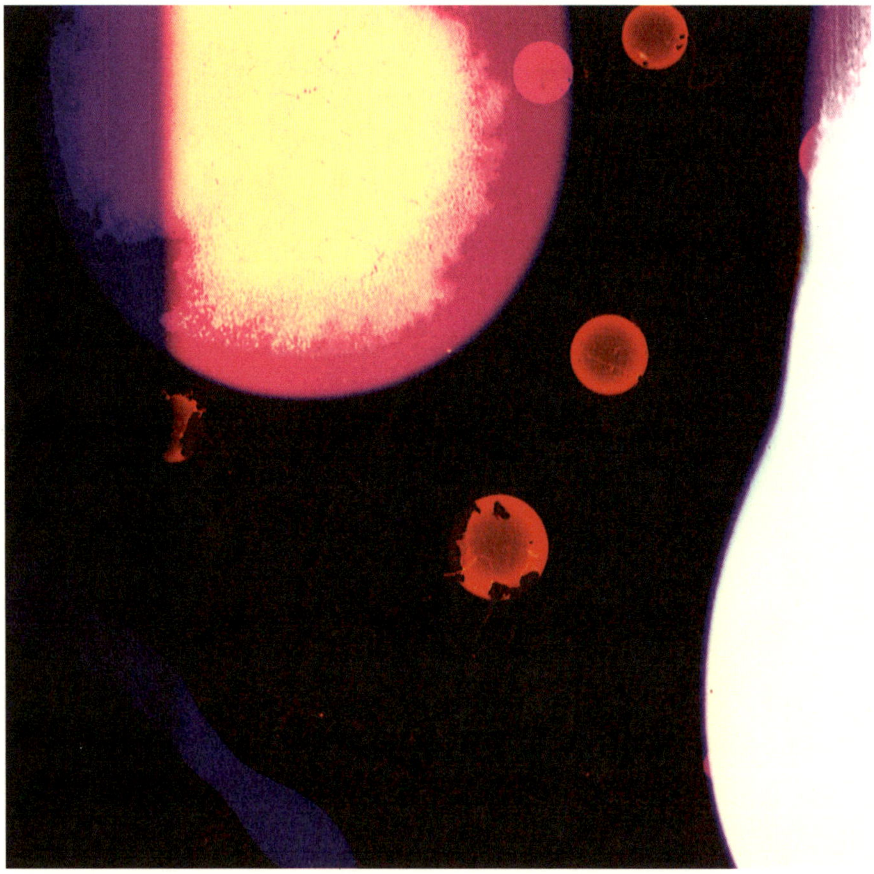

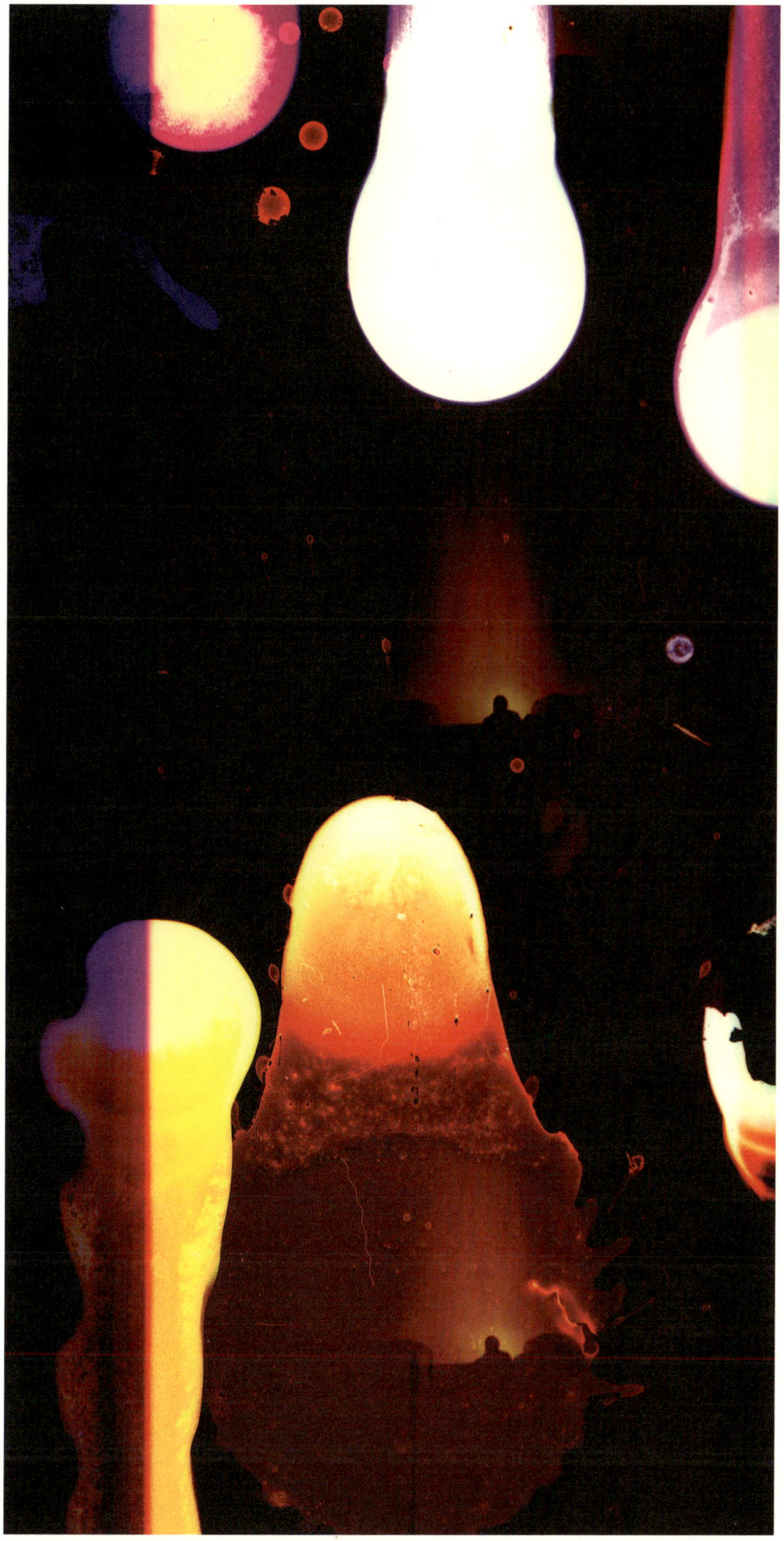

Jennifer West, *Electric Kool-Aid Fountain Swimming Film (35 mm movie negative submerged in LA's Mulholland Fountain, dripped with Kool-Aid and liquid LSD – featuring nighttime fountain swimming by Mateo Tannatt, Lia Trinka-Brownwe, Lesley Moon, Mariah Csepanyi and Jwest)*, 2008

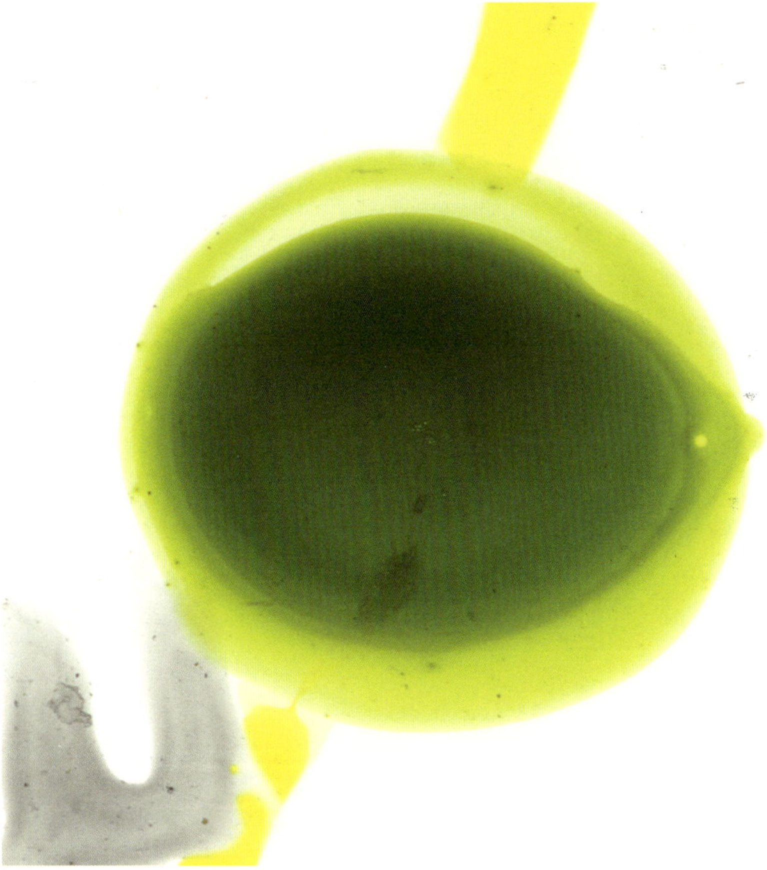

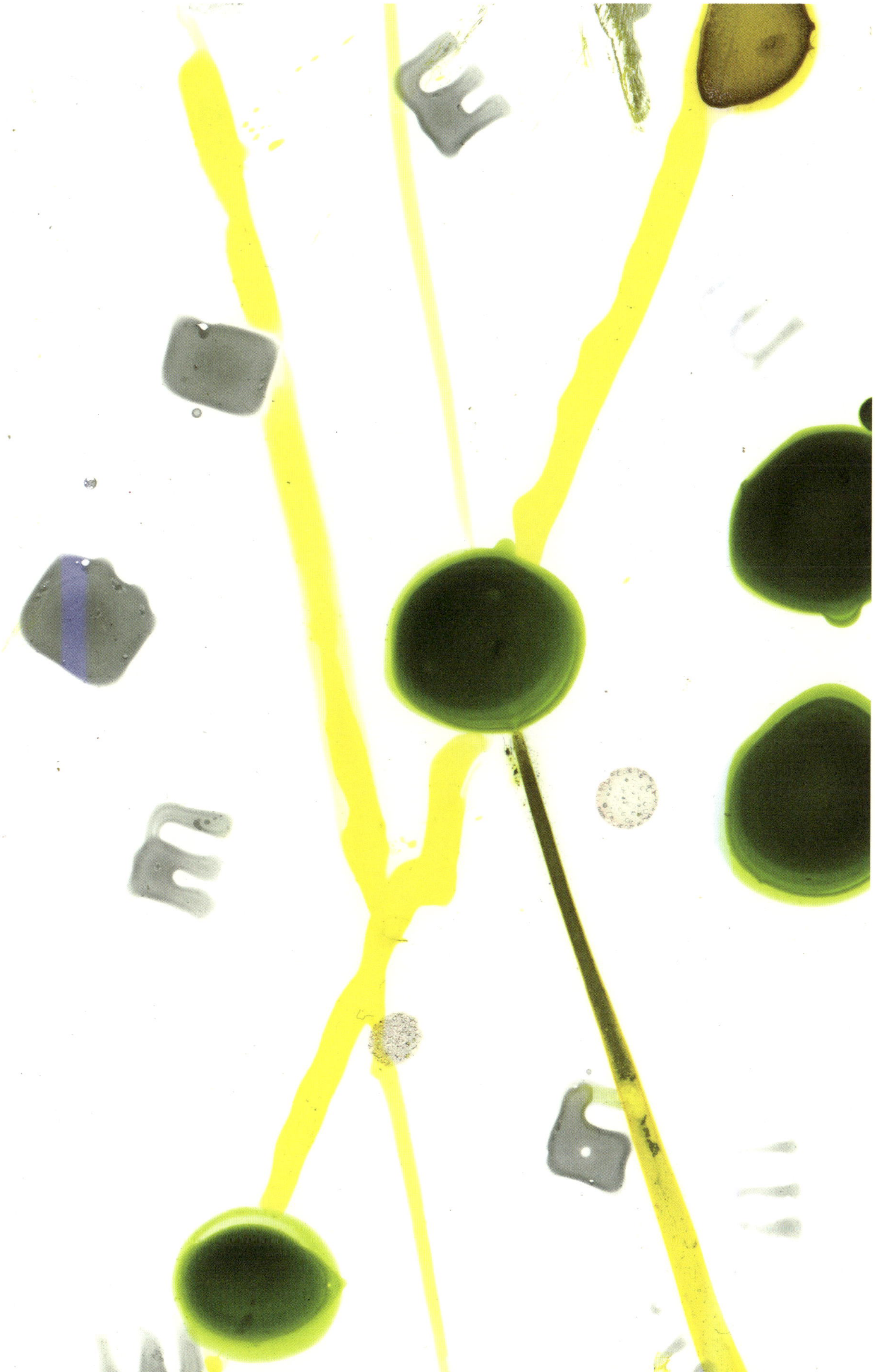

Jennifer West, *Green M&M's and Mezcal Worm Film (70 mm film leader with a mescal worm dragged over the surface – imprinted with hundreds of green M & Ms)*, 2008

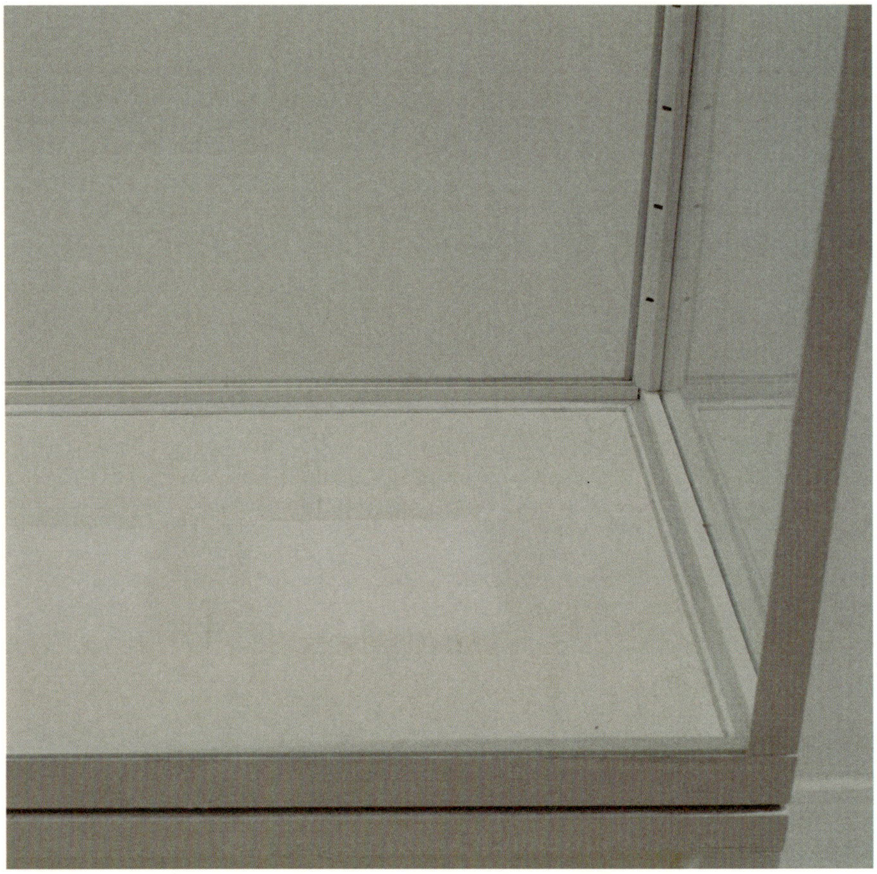

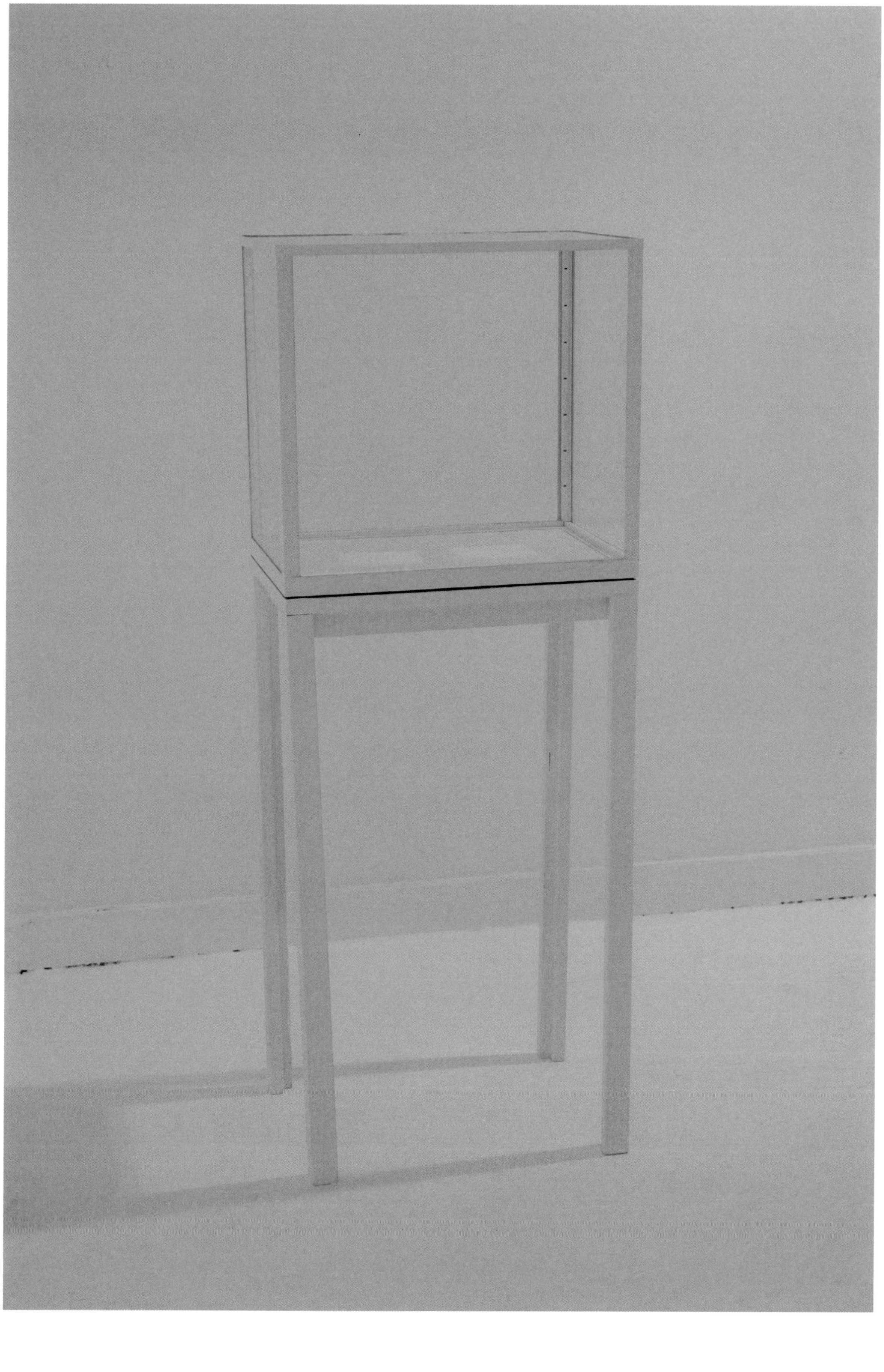

Erwin Wurm, *Dust Piece*, 1991

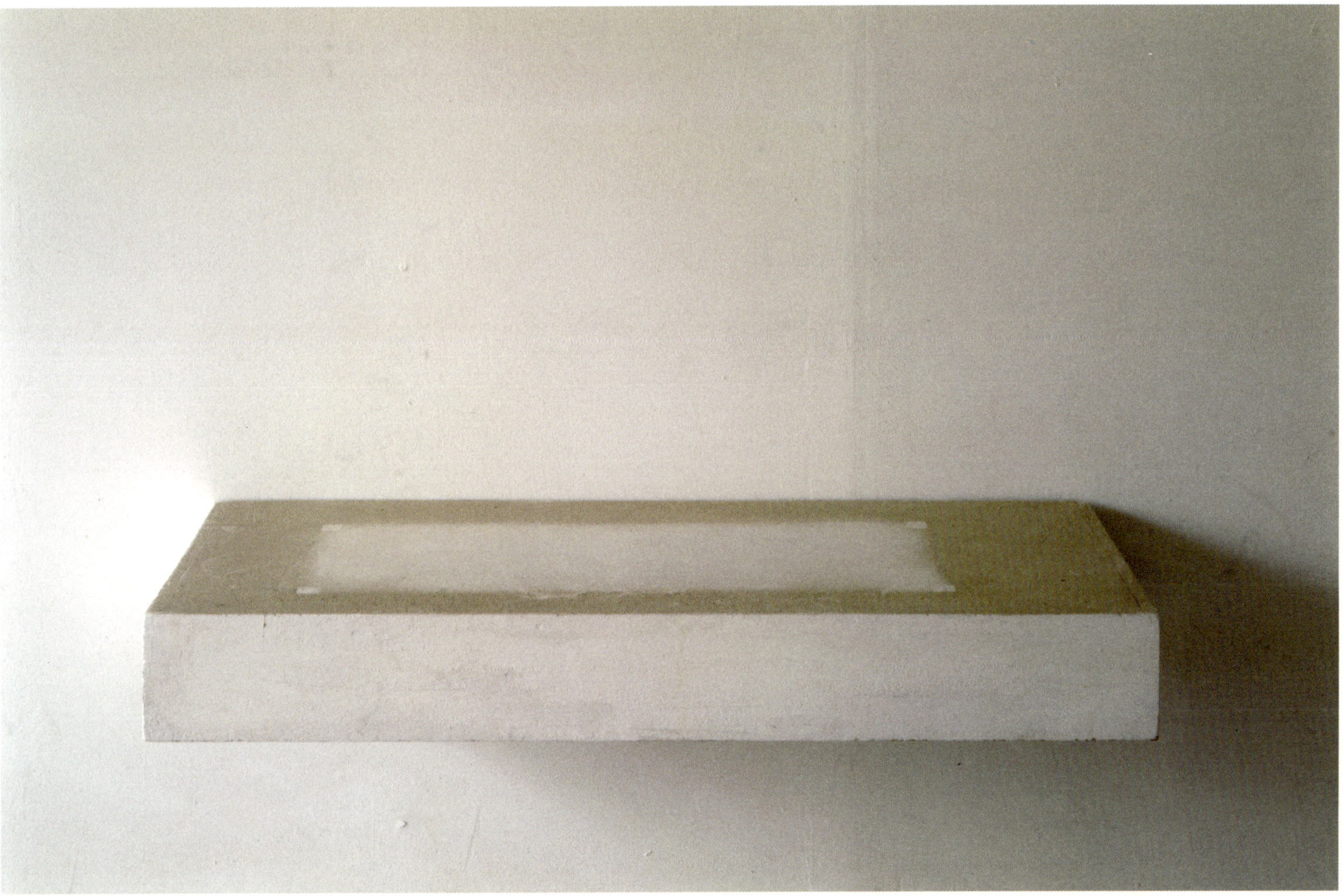

Erwin Wurm, *Untitled (Dust Piece)*, 1991

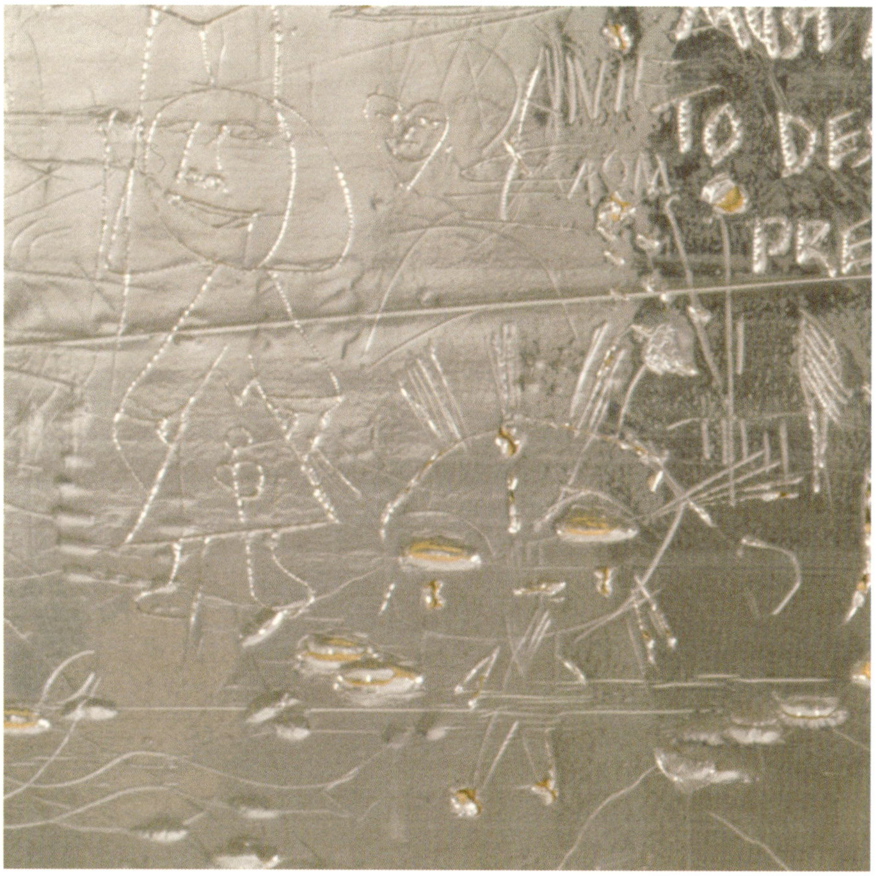

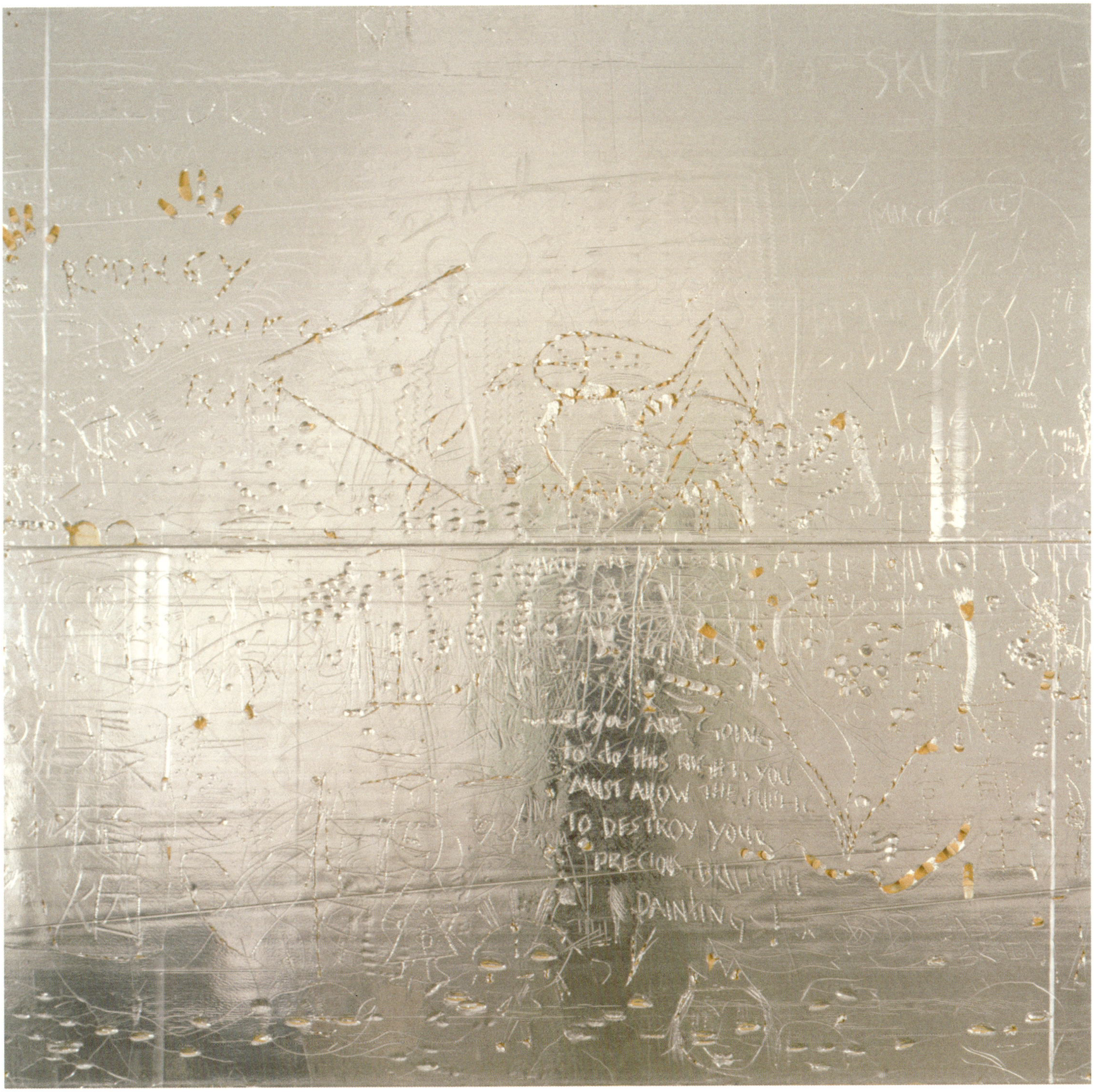

Rudolf Stingel, *Untitled*, 2002

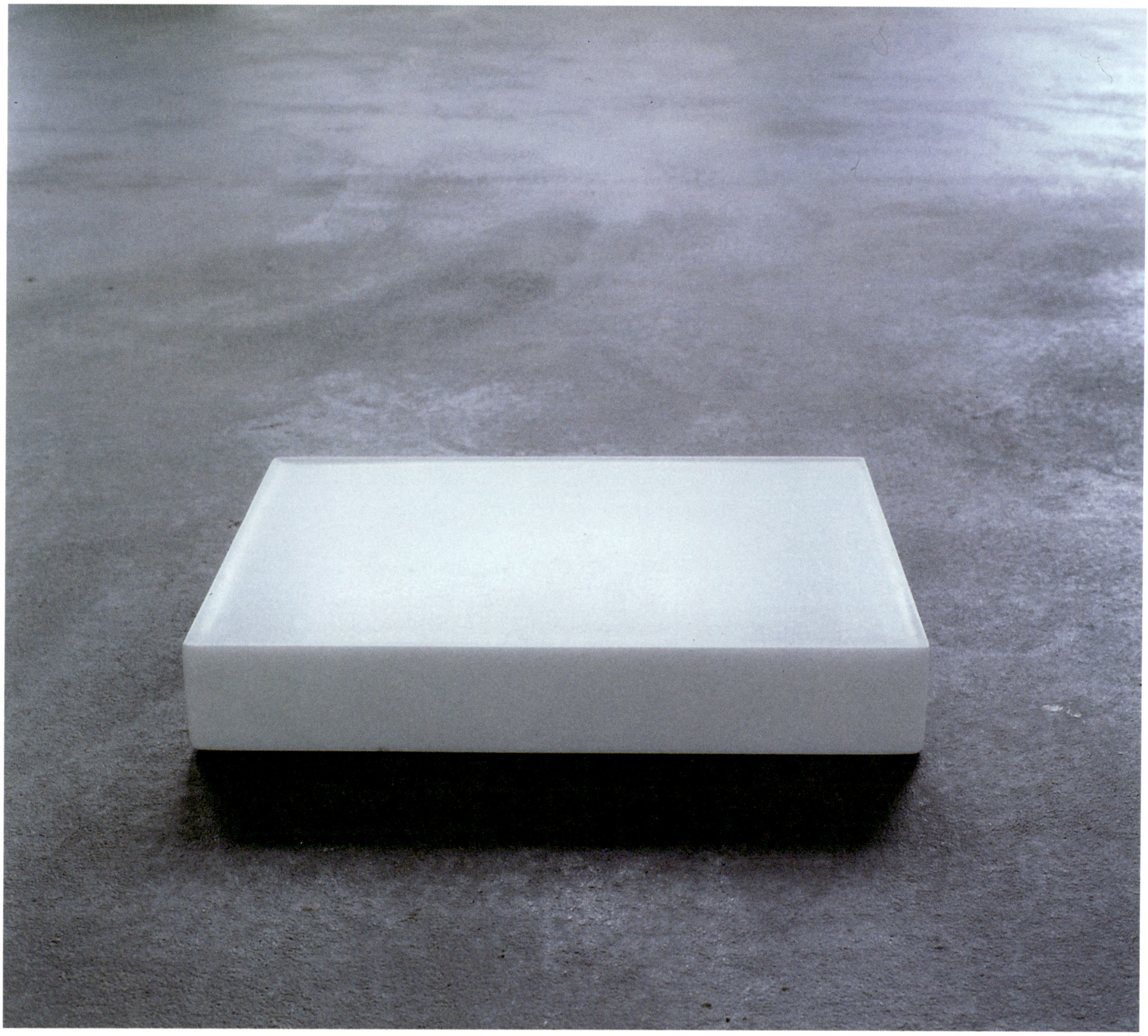

Wolfgang Laib, *Milkstone*, 1997

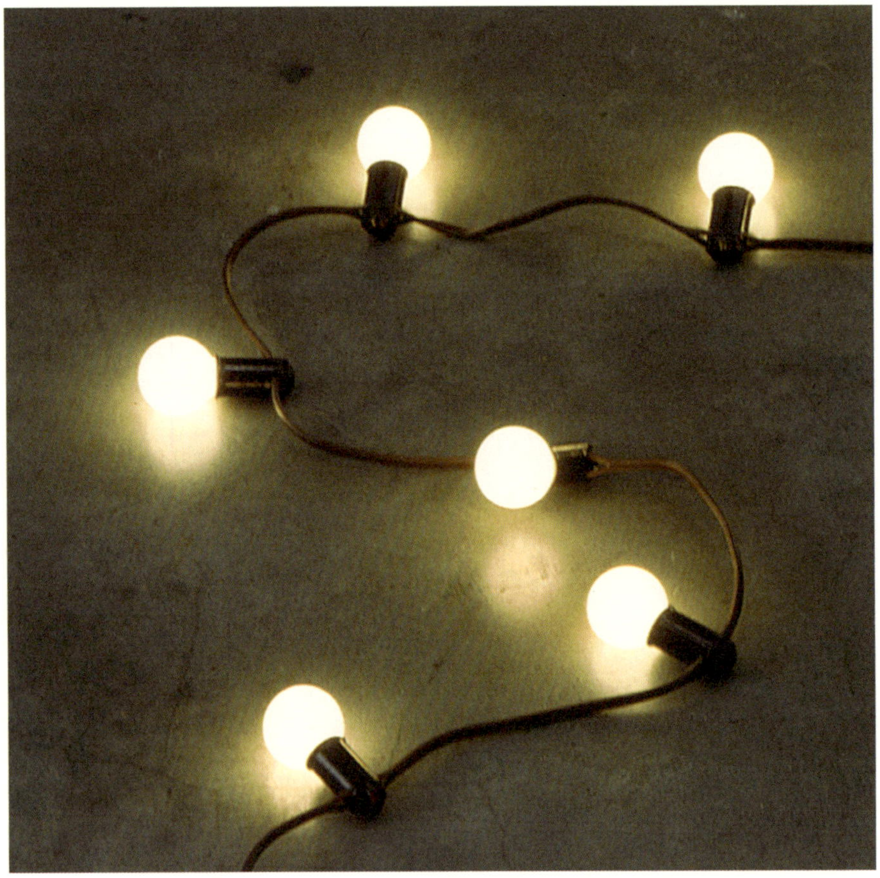

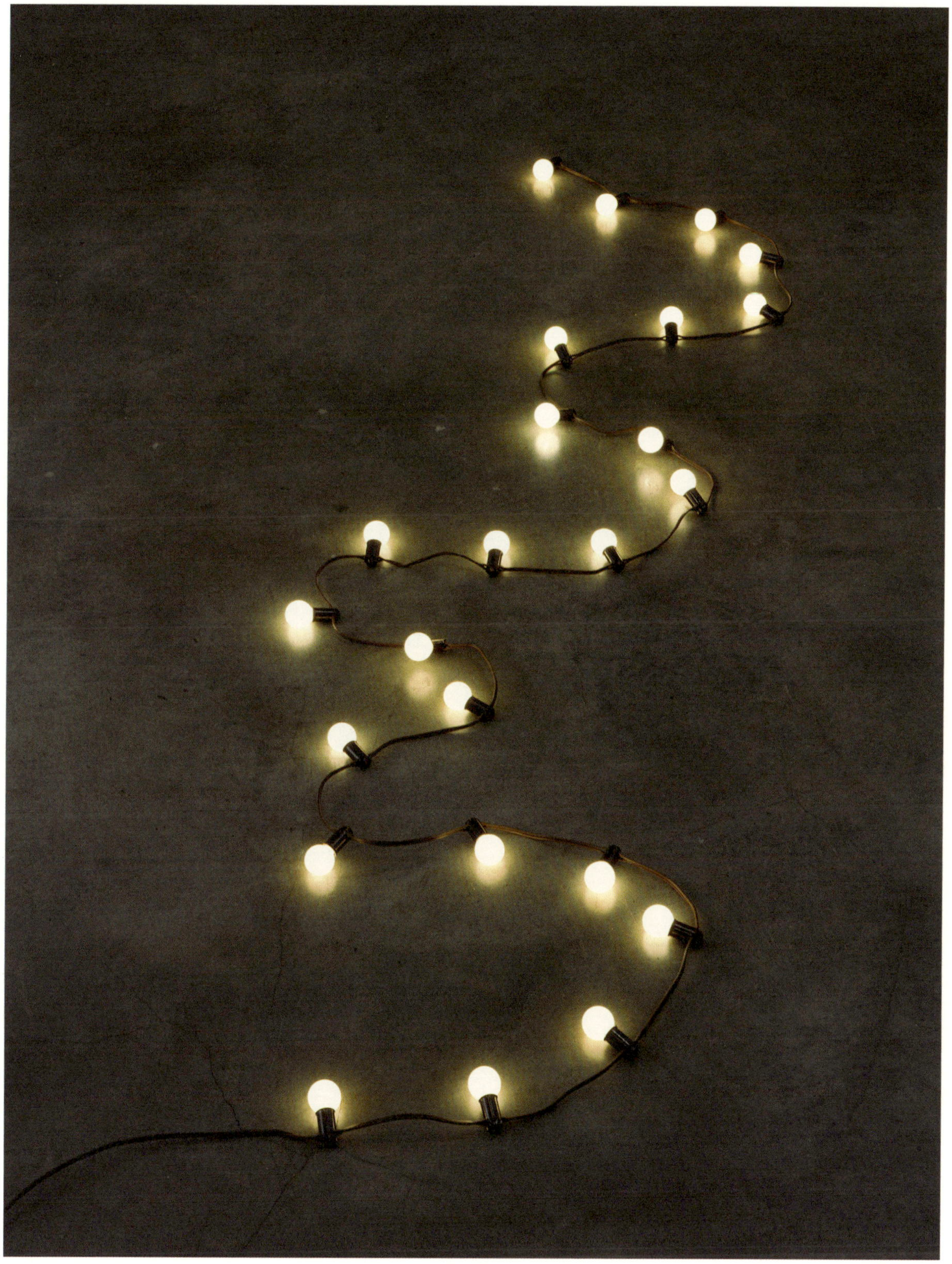

Felix Gonzalez-Torres, *"Untitled" (Last Light)*, 1993

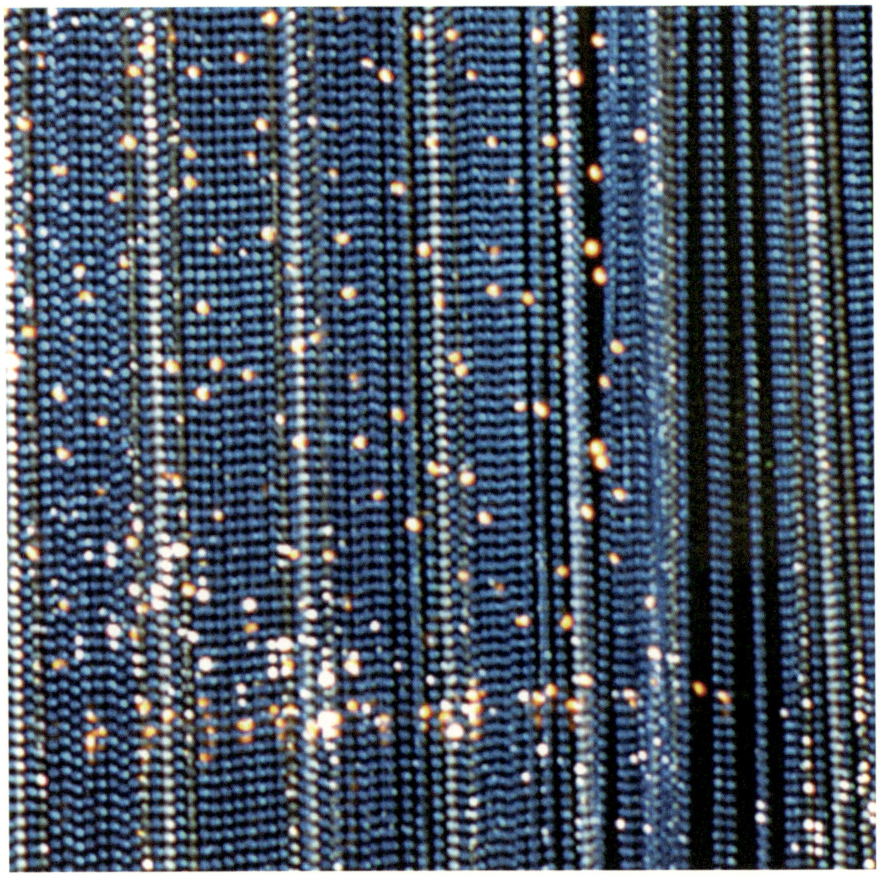

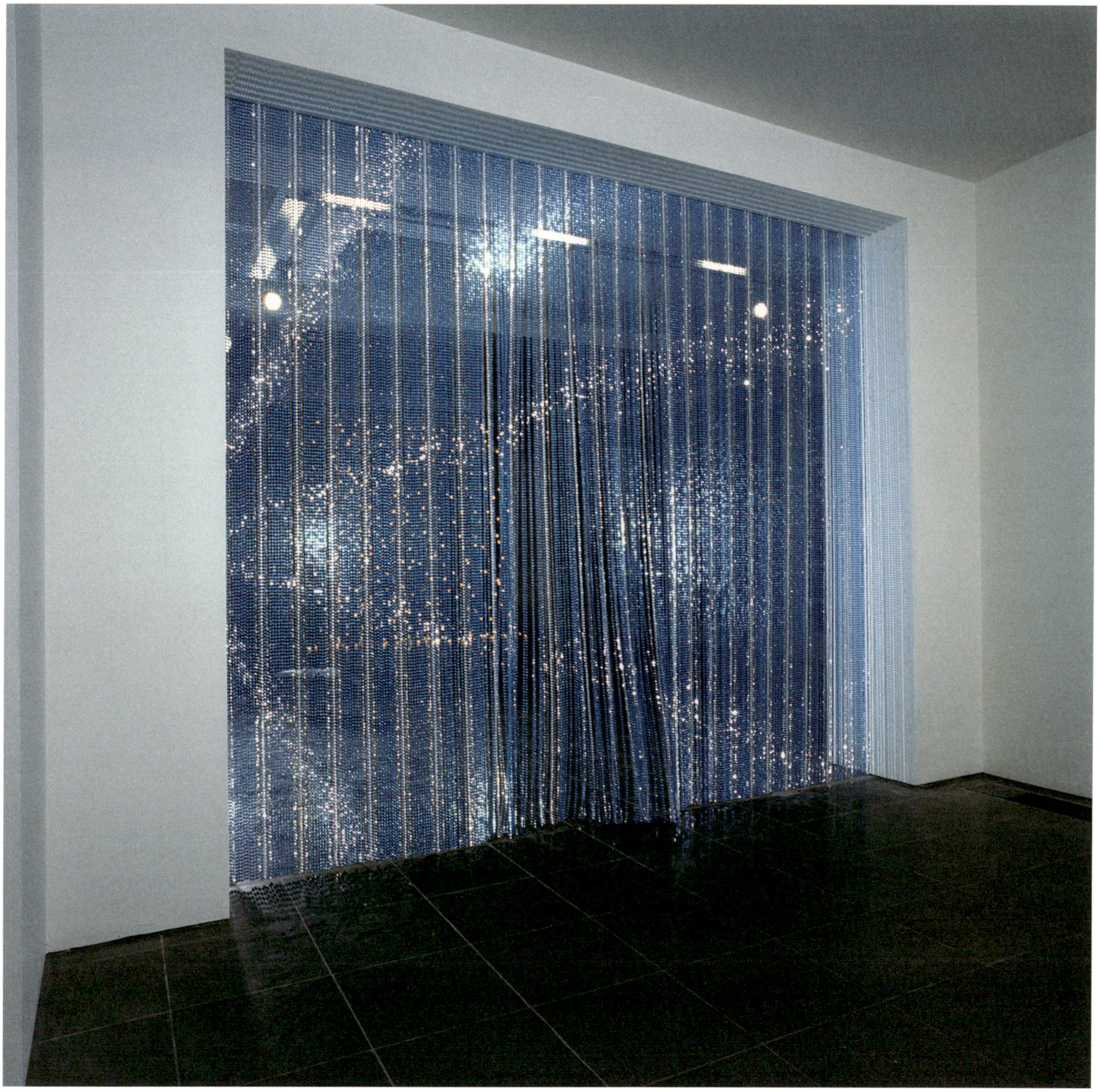

Felix Gonzalez-Torres, *"Untitled" (Water)*, 1995

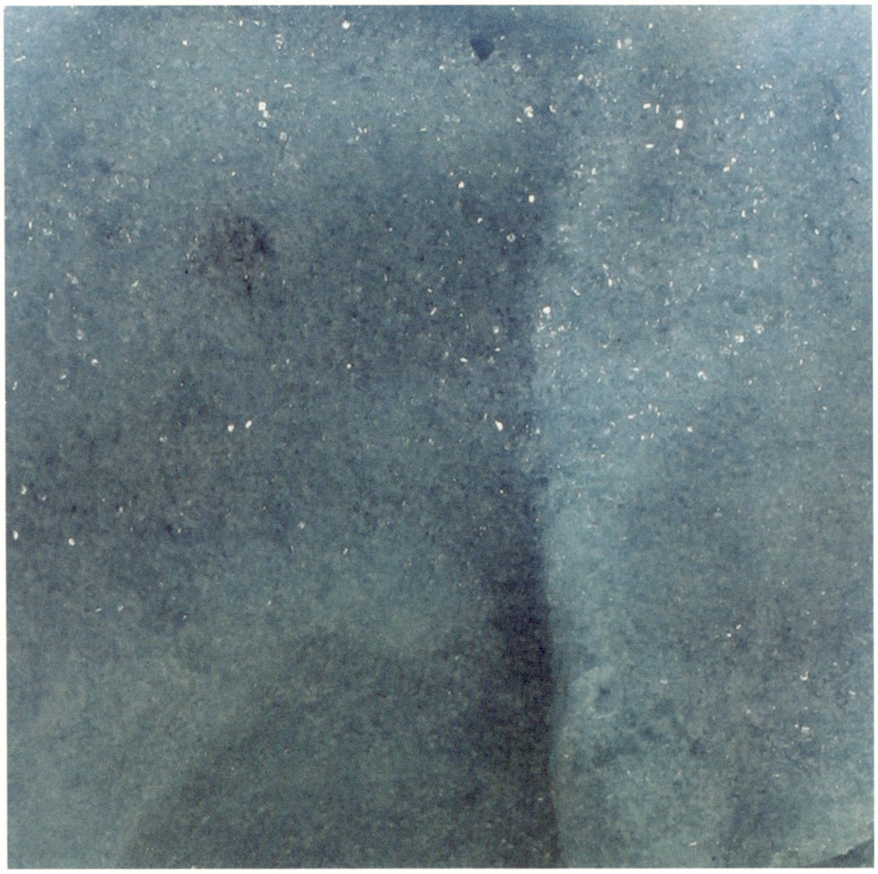

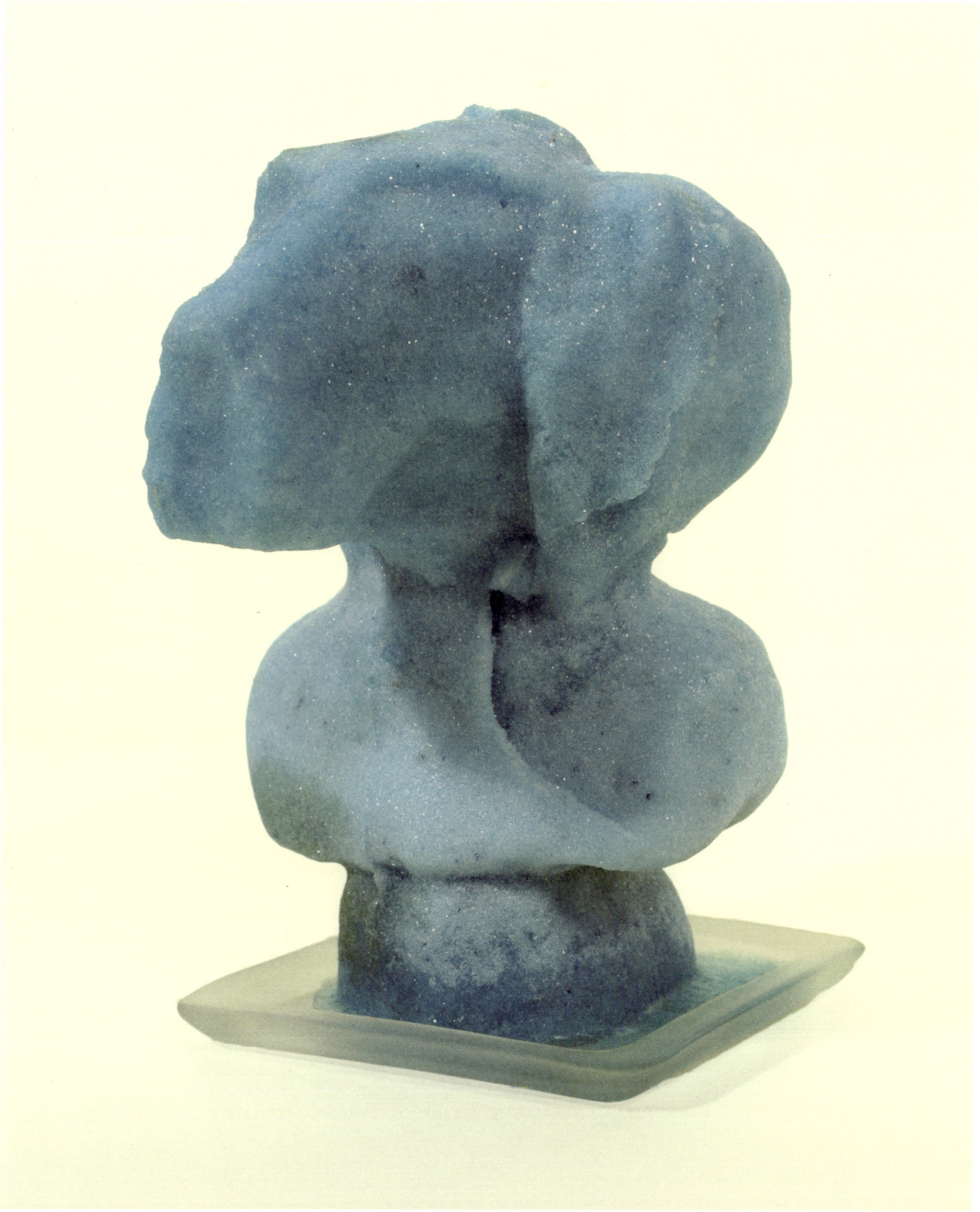

Dieter Roth, *Lion Bust*, 1961

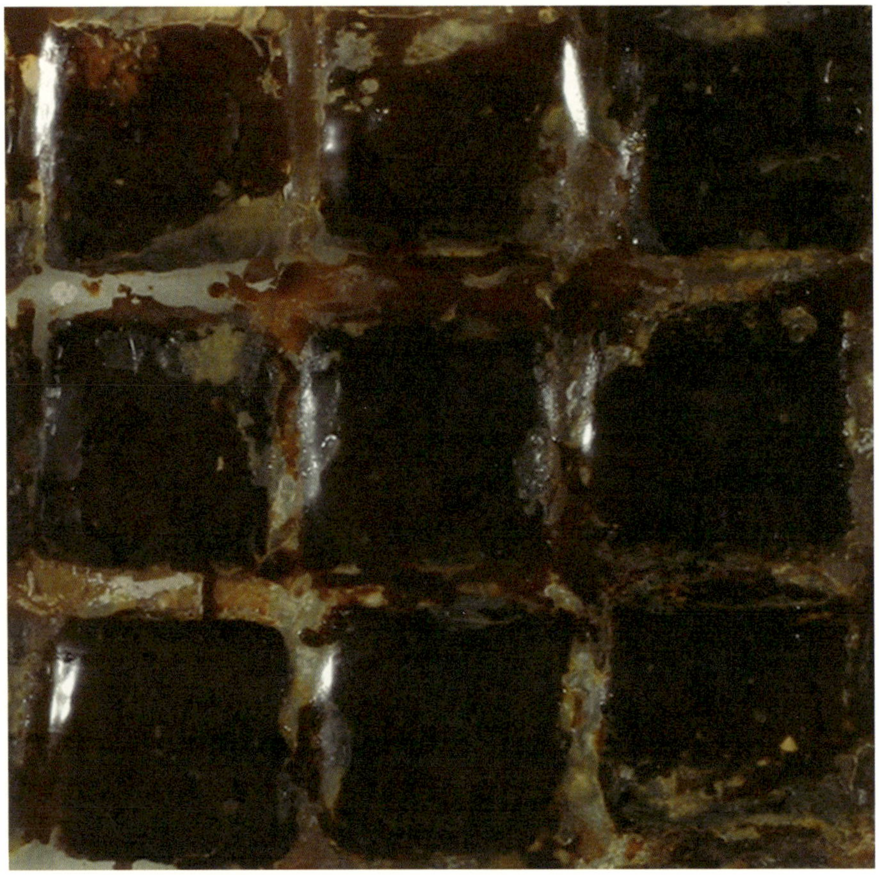

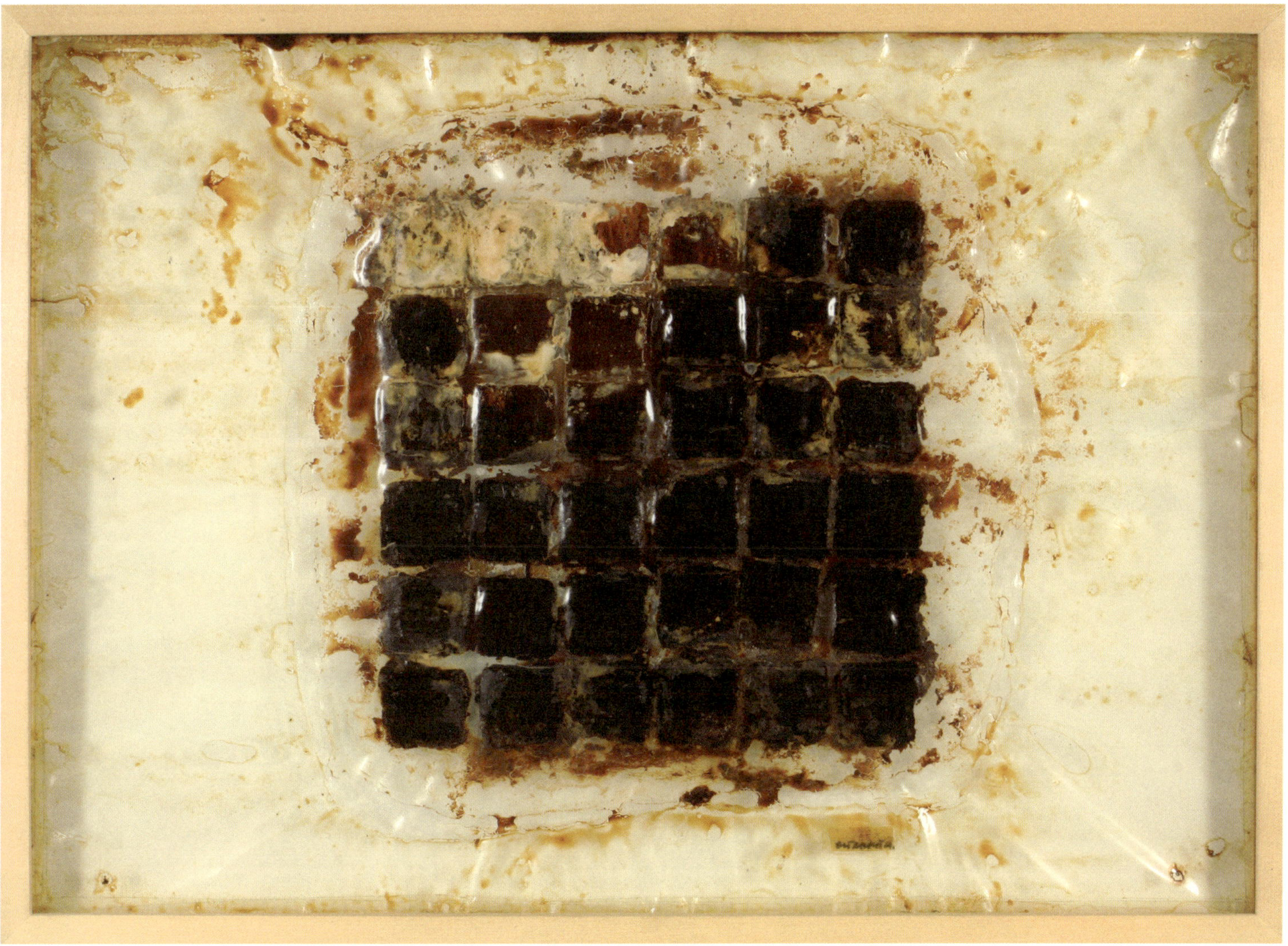

Dieter Roth, *Schokoladenplätzchenbild (chocolate wafer picture)*, 1969

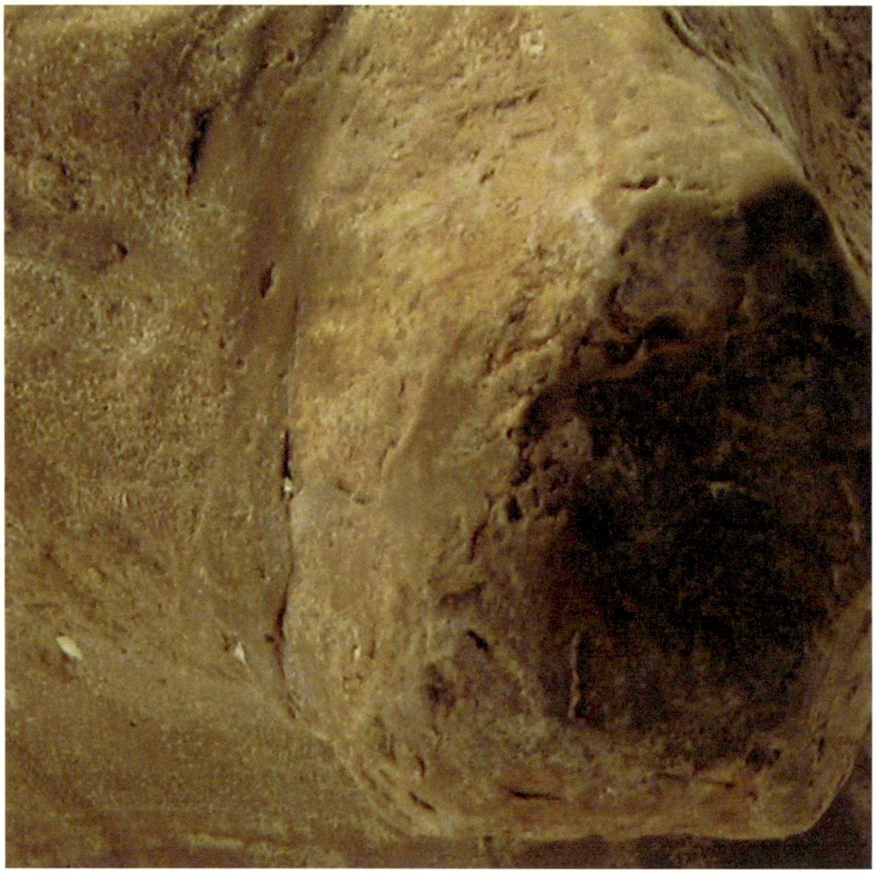

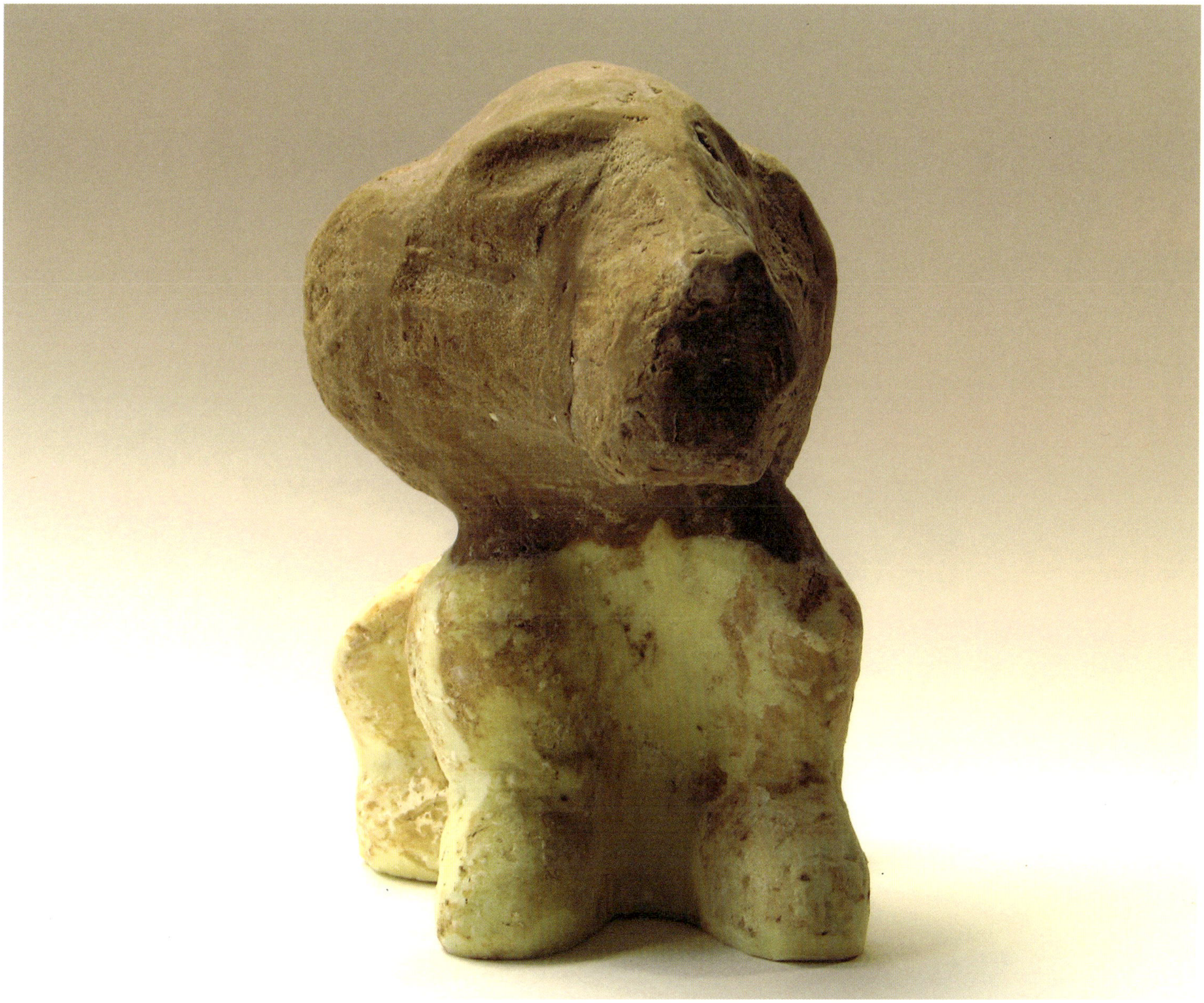

Dieter Roth, *Schokoladenlowe,* 1969–89

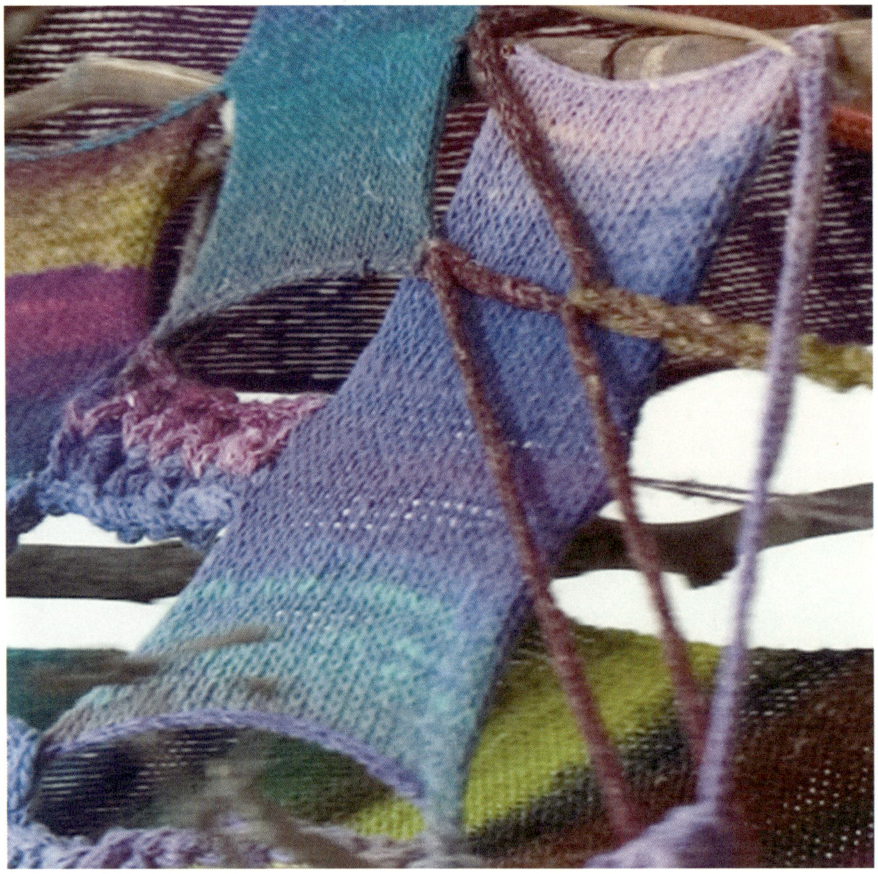

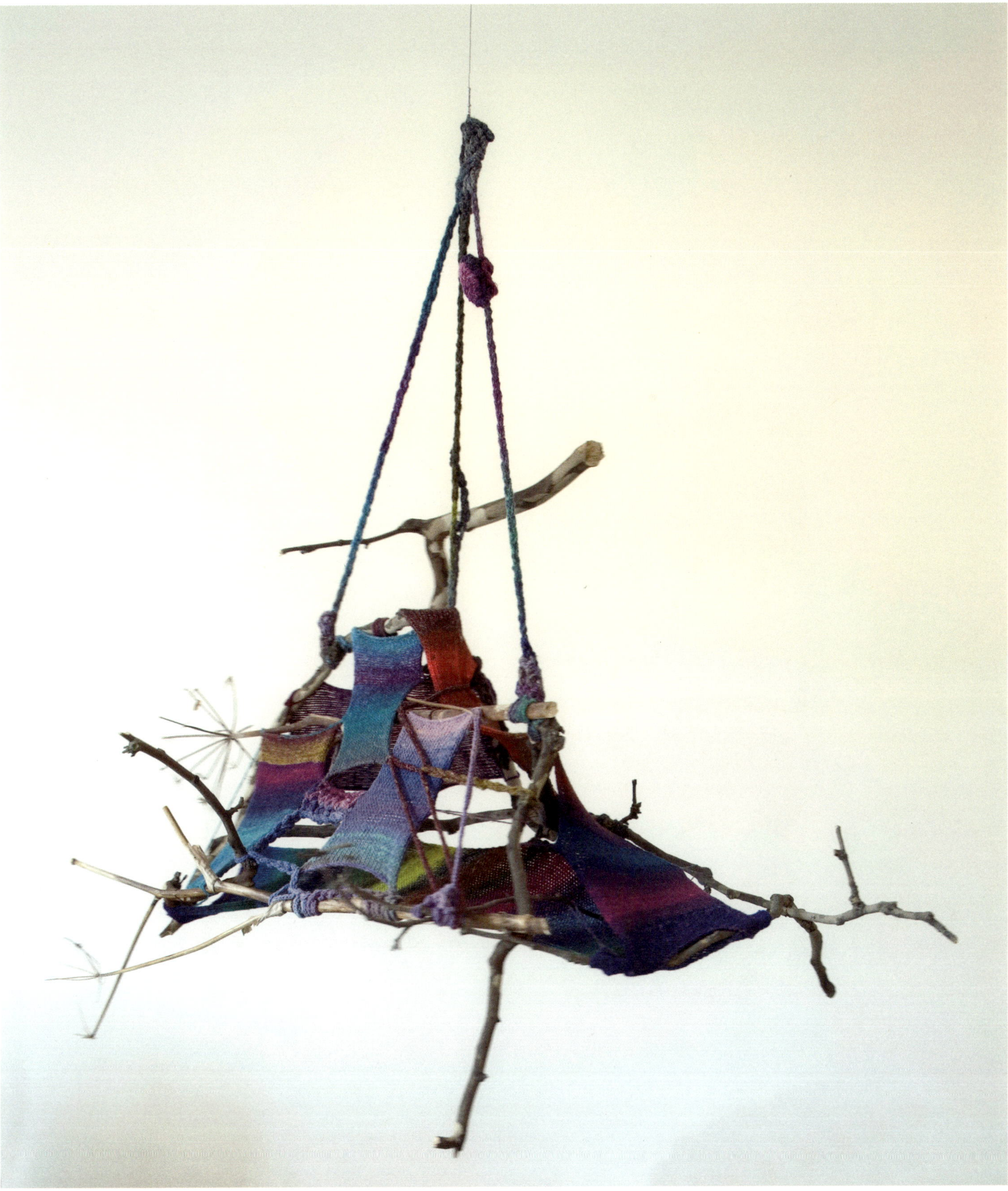

Alexandra Bircken, *Ship*, 2007

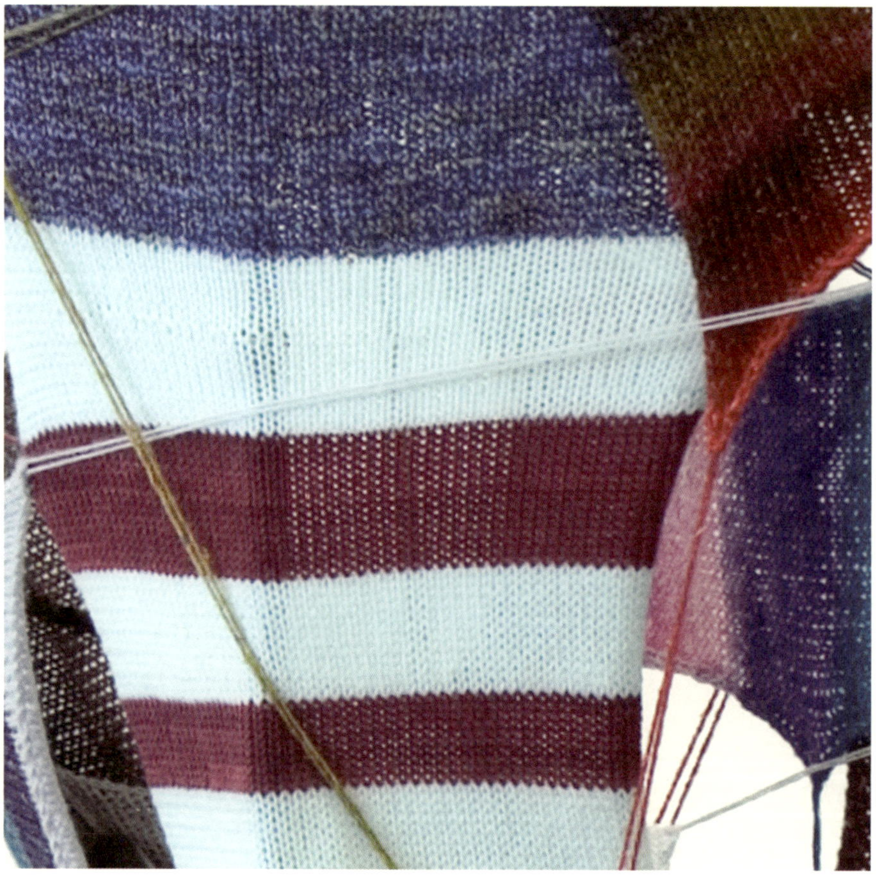

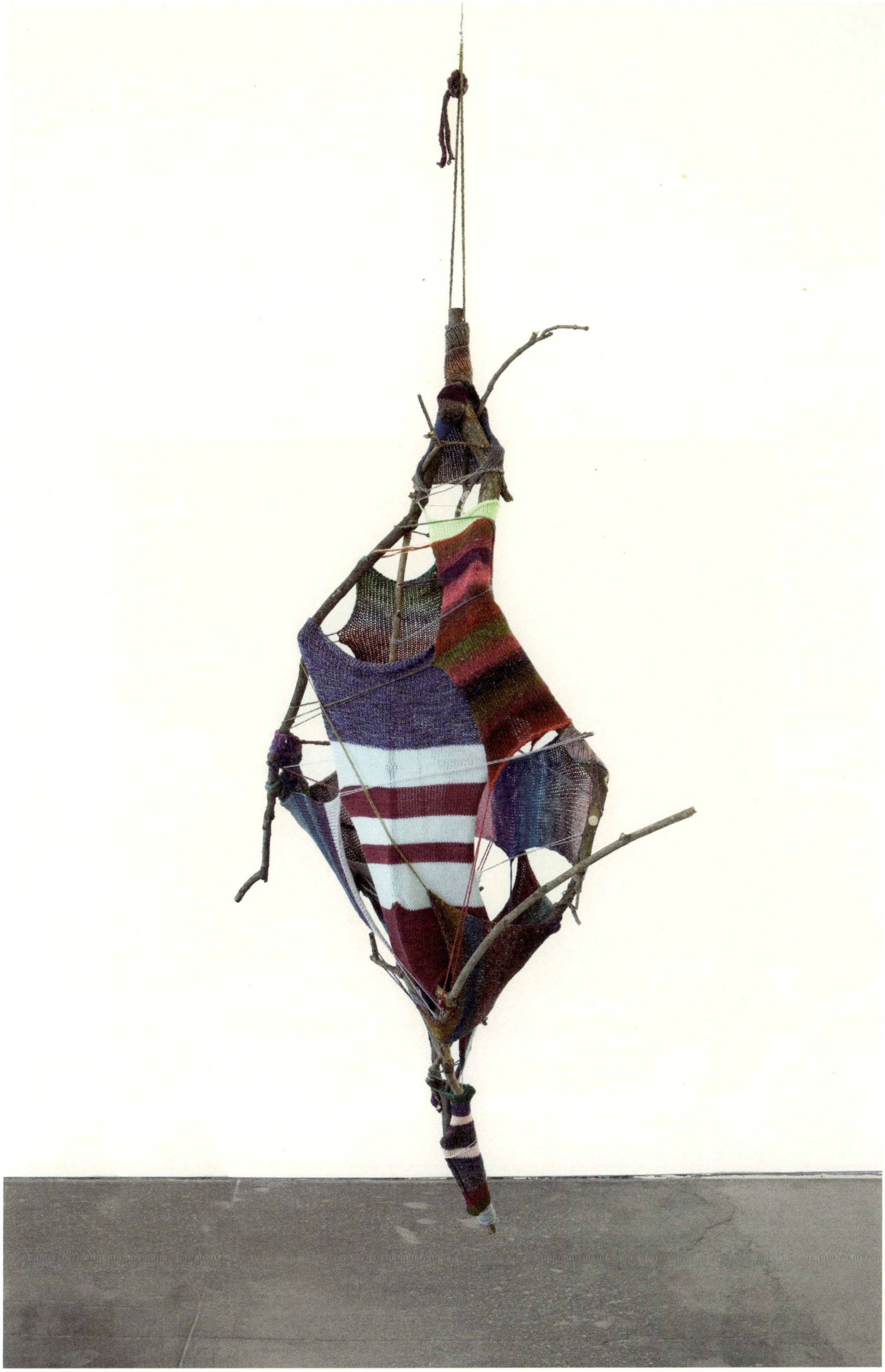

Alexandra Bircken, *Spindel*, 2007

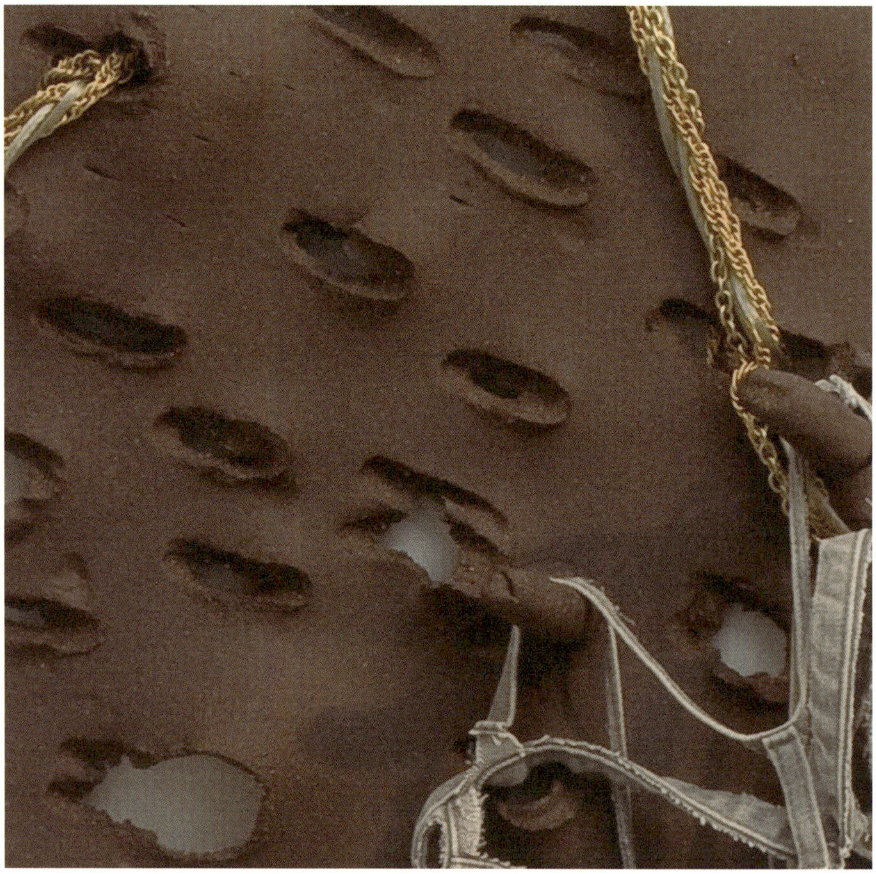

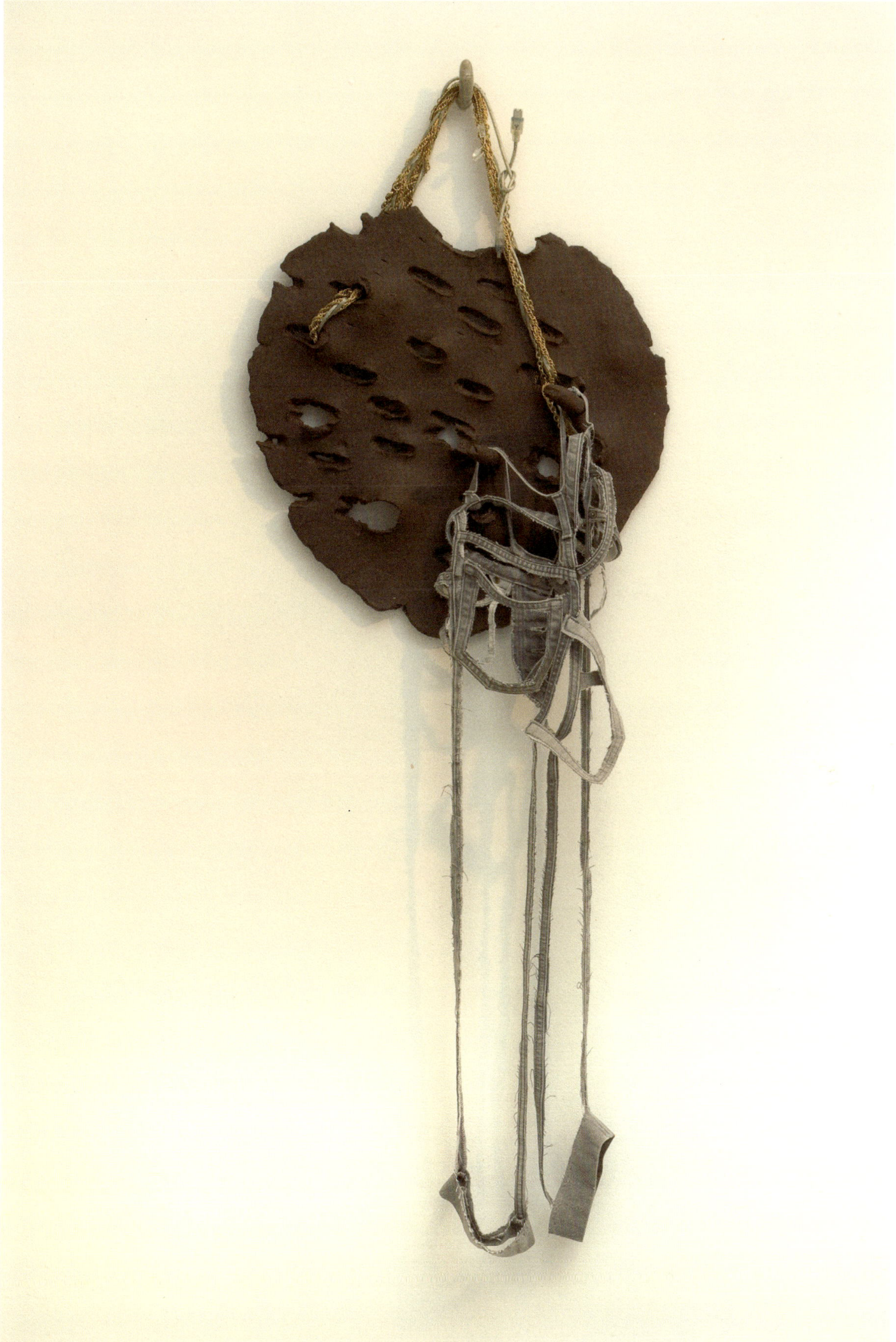

Anna Sew Hoy, *Heart*, 2007

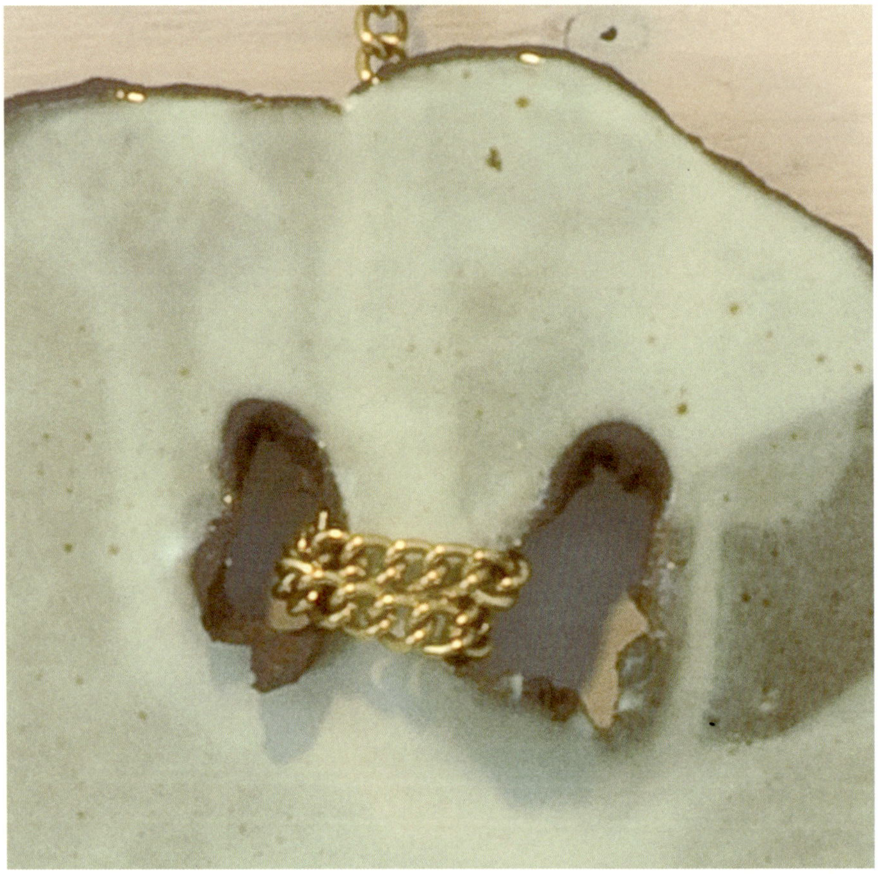

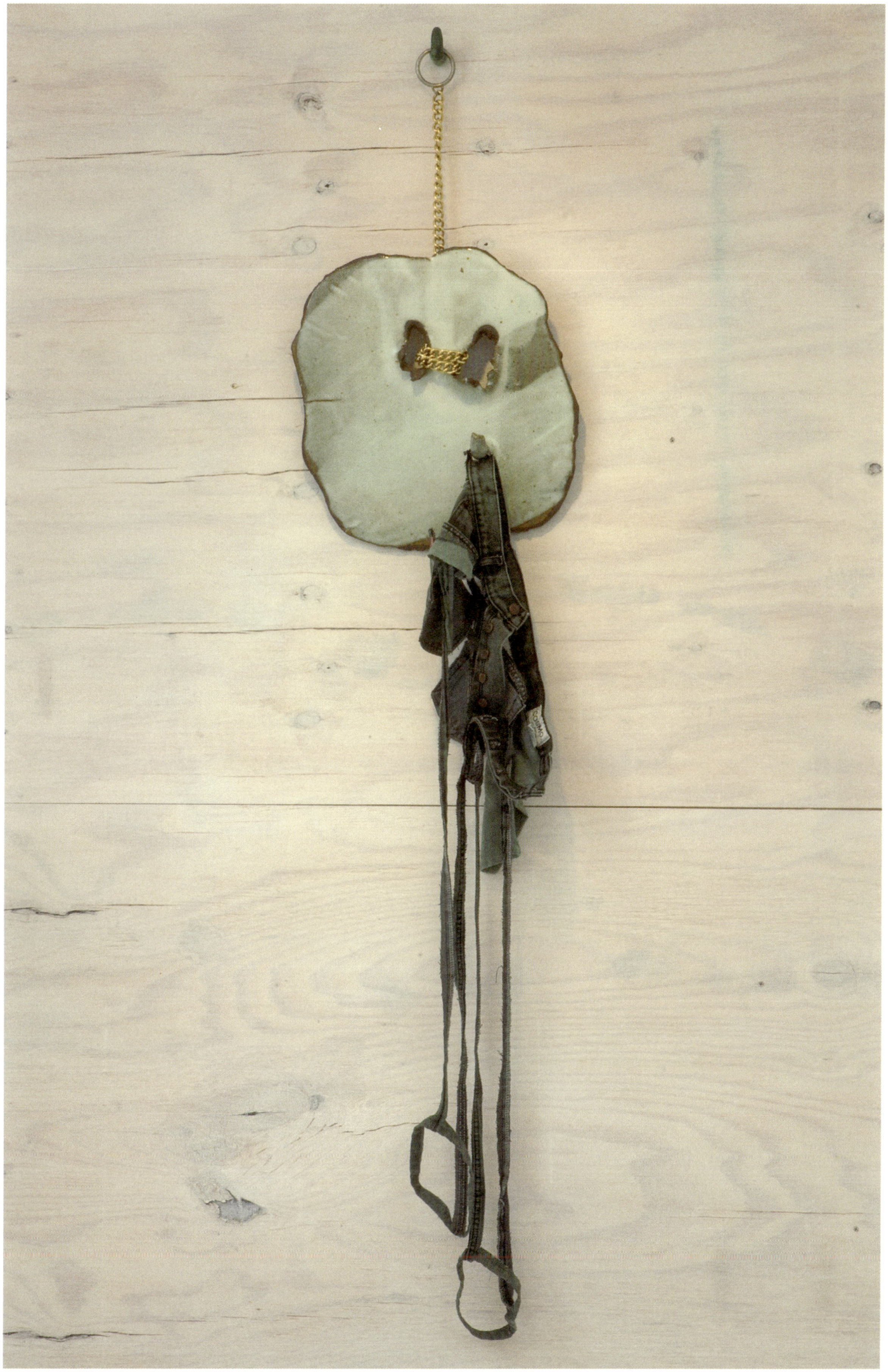

Anna Sew Hoy, *Two Eyes*, 2007

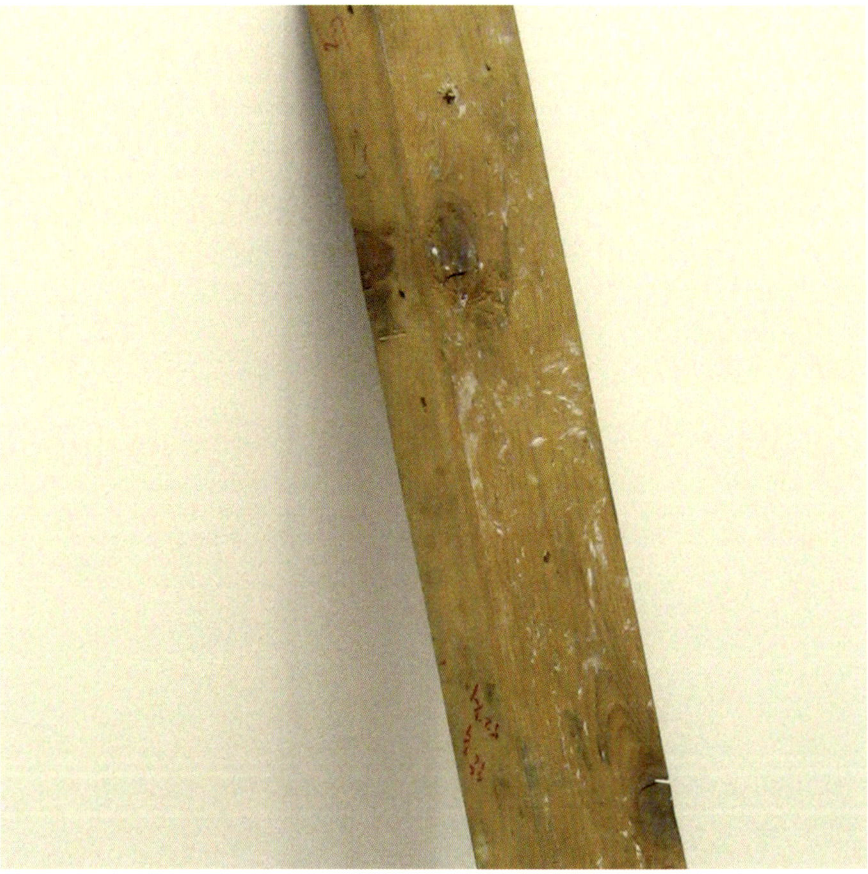

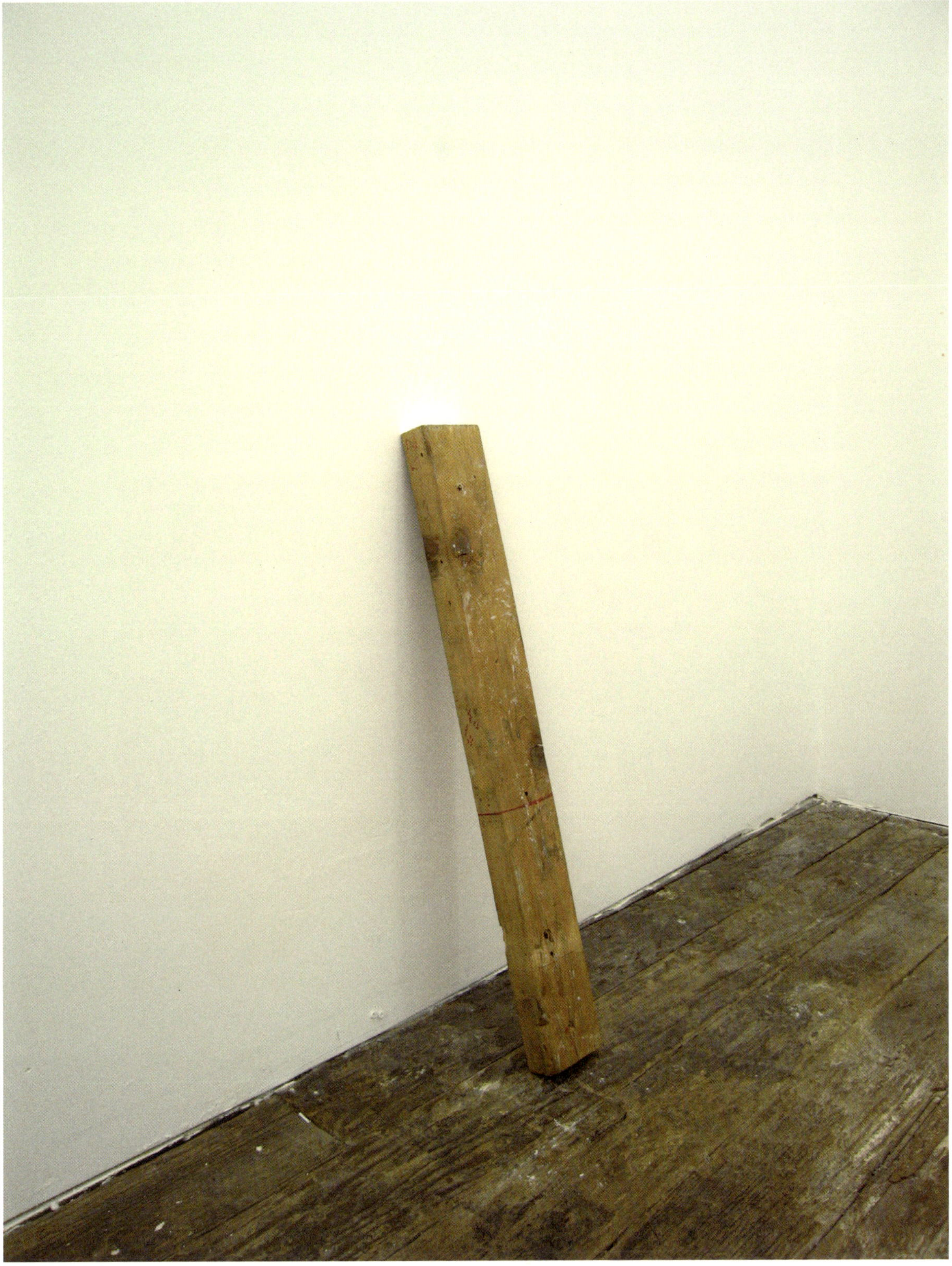

Mitzi Pederson, *Untitled*, 2008

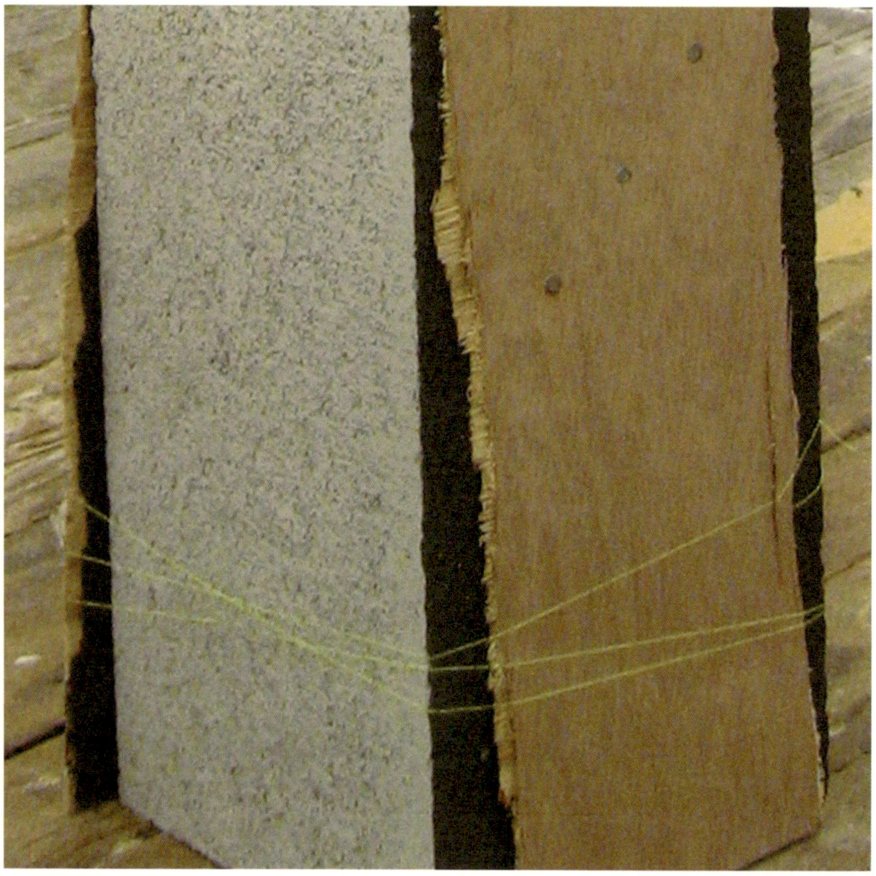

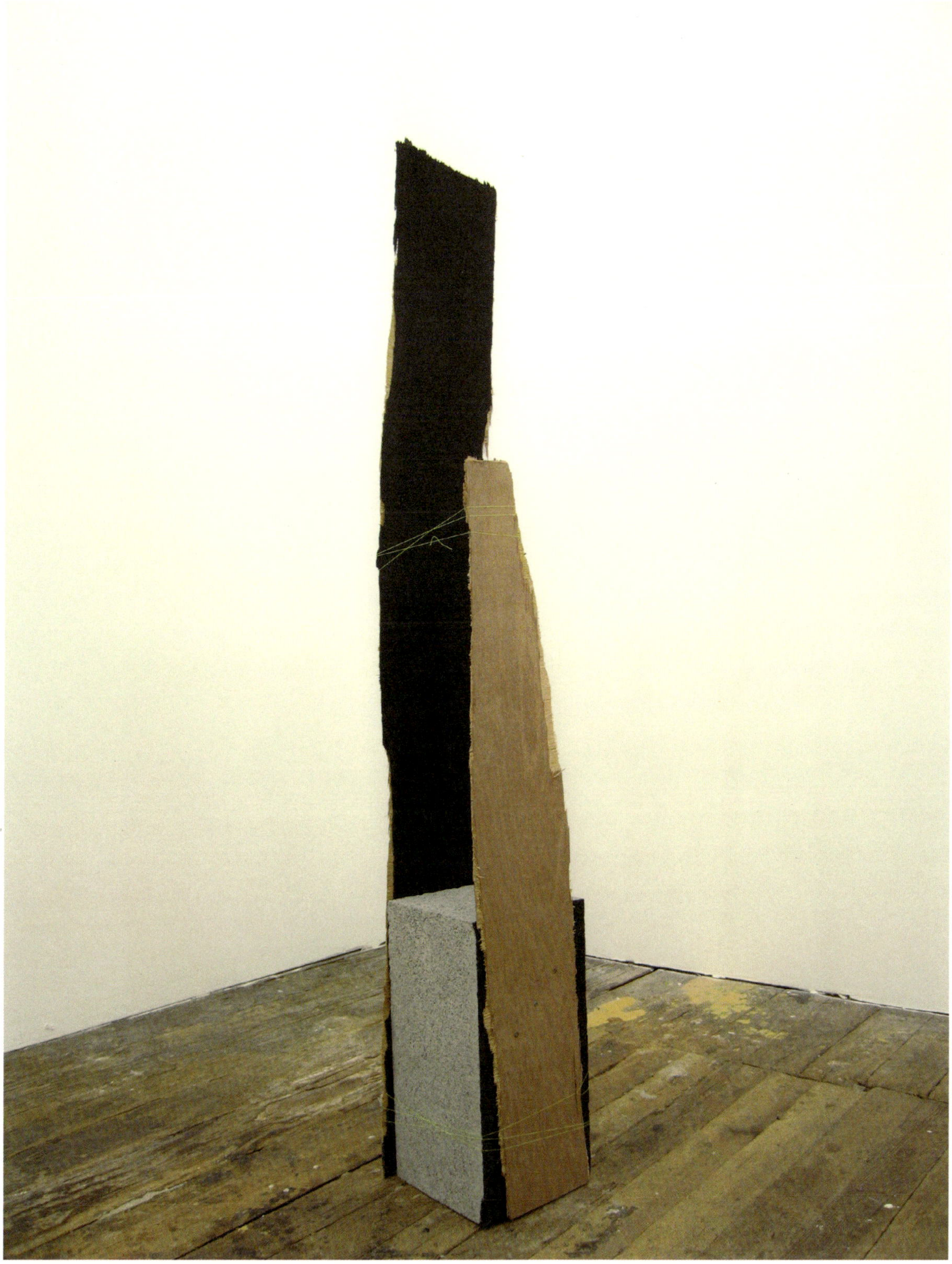

Mitzi Pederson, *Untitled*, 2008

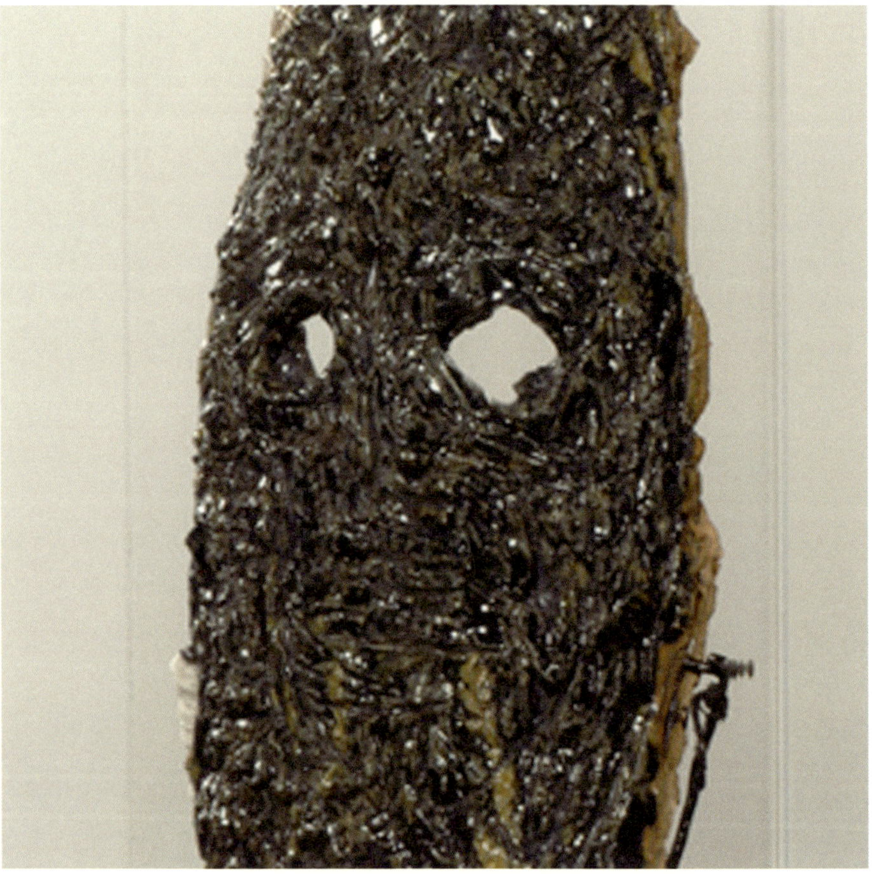

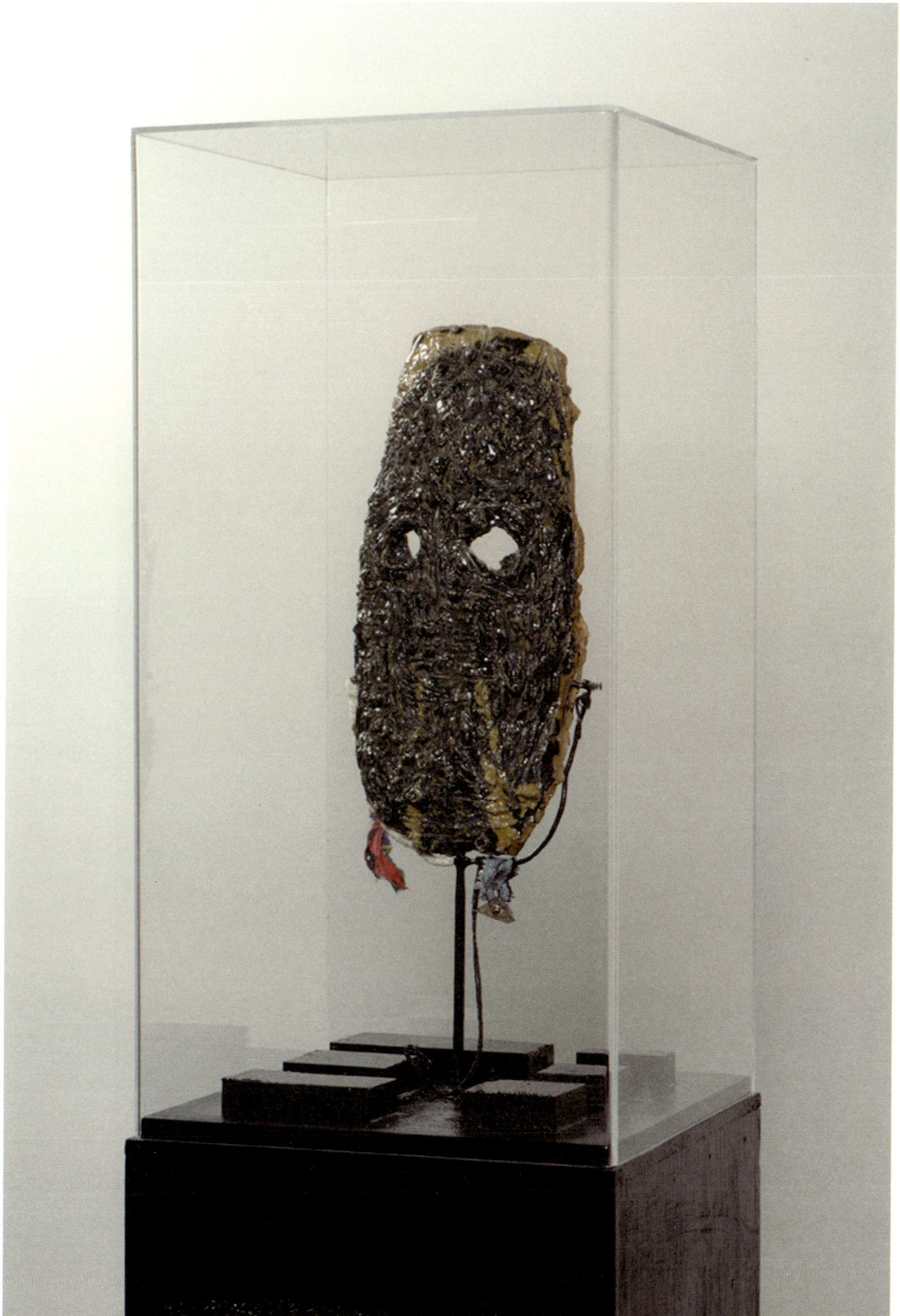

William O'Brien, *Untitled,* 2008

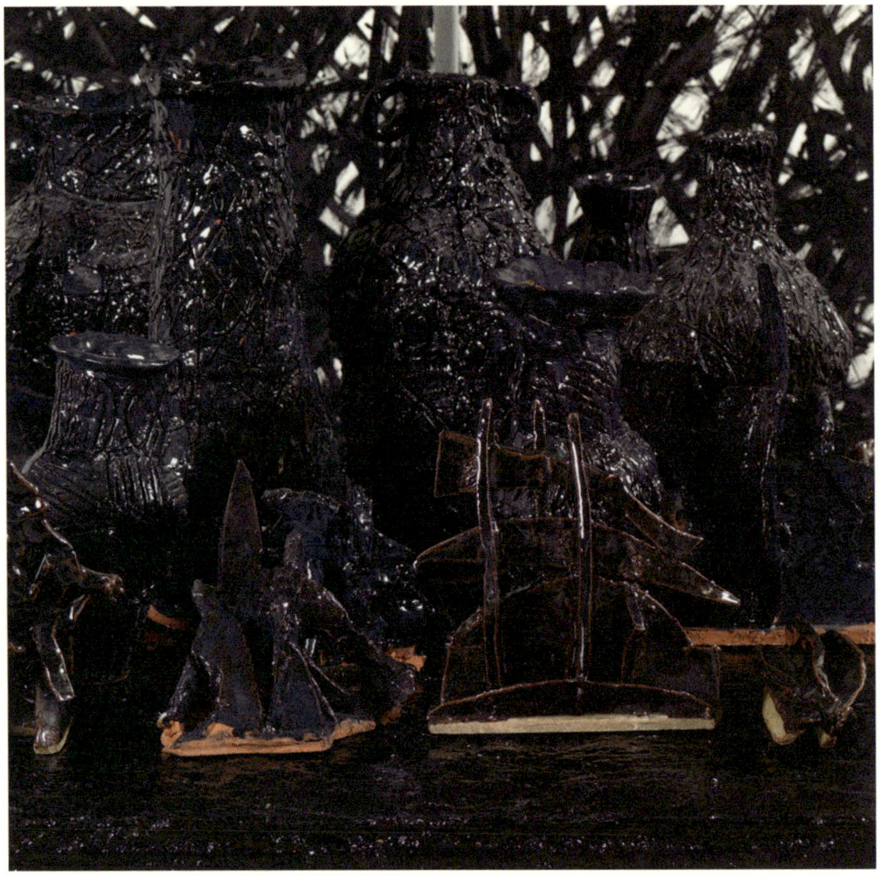

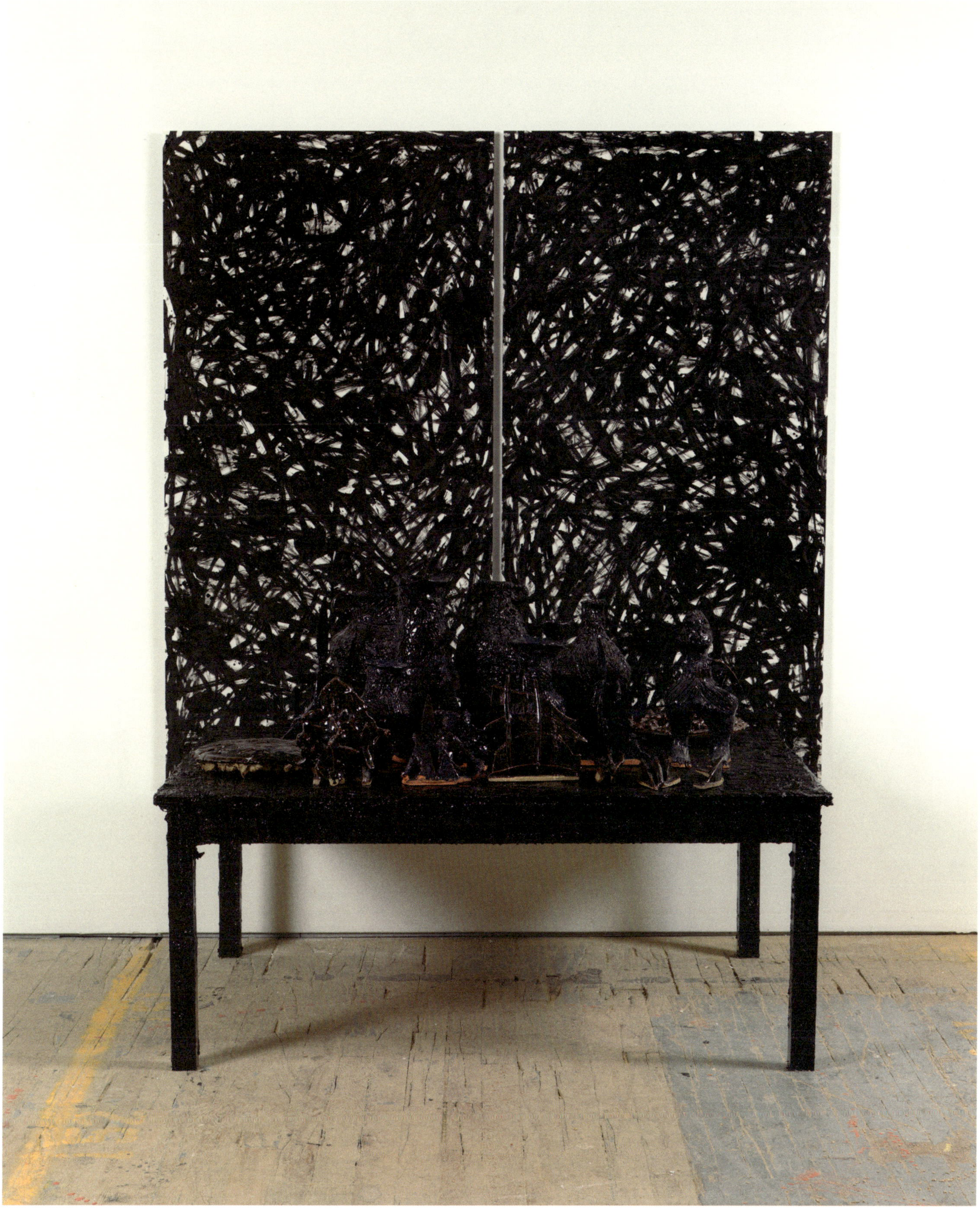

William O'Brien, *Untitled,* 2008

Selected Excerpts from a Conversation Between Felix Gonzalez-Torres and Tim Rollins

"With the new work, the light-strings, I leave those decisions for others to perform. I don't decide how the strings of lights are installed, I only specify that the piece must have forty-two twenty-watt light bulbs." (8-9)

[Discussing Althusser, Barthes, Benjamin, Borges, and Foucault] "Some of their writings and ideas gave me a certain freedom to see. These ideas moved me to a place of pleasure through knowledge and some understanding of the way reality is constructed, of the way the self is formed in culture, of the way language sets traps, and of the cracks in the 'master narrative' – those cracks where power can be exercised. It is also about influences and role models." (10)

"We are supposed to 'feel,' not think. Brecht says to keep a distance to allow the viewer, the public, time to reflect and think. When you get out of the theater you should not have had a catharsis, you should have had a thinking experience. More than anything, break the pleasure of representation, the pleasure of the flawless narrative. This is not life, this is just a theater piece. I like that a lot: *This is not life, this is just an artwork.* I want you, the viewer, to be intellectually challenged, moved, and informed." (10-11)

"It is very exciting to take something that is there in everyday life and create from it something out of the ordinary, to give that ordinary object or situation a new meaning with a great economy of means." (18)

"I'm for pushing the limits. I love it when people say: 'But it is just paper. It is just two clocks next to each other. It is just light bulbs hanging.' I love the idea of being an infiltrator. I always said that I wanted to be a spy. I want my artwork to look like something else, non-artistic yet beautifully simple. I don't want to be the opposition because the opposition always serves a purpose: 'Improve your arms against me.'" (20-21)

"But aside from the objects, I love the process more than that final product. That's what I love the most. But I understand the rules of the game: you have to circulate an object in the market in order to have a more direct access to power..." (27)

"I think happiness comes from knowing what you want to do. I don't want to discuss the objects that much. I think the issues, the processes, the needs, and the pleasures around the works are more important." (27)

"It's based on the Brechtian model. It is not about good or bad. You try to give them the ability, the tools, to see for themselves what is important, what is needed, what is moving, and what is not. I also make very clear to them that they should not trust me—I'm not the voice of authority. I make mistakes, I might be wrong. I do have a very clear agenda and that is a desire to make this place a better place, and I'm an artist, that is the position where I speak from. But I'm an artist who tries to redefine the role of the artist." (28)

Tim: "So what role does art play in that?"

Felix: "It leaves a mark. It leaves a statement that you were here, that perhaps it is possible to have a different view of life." (30)

Originally printed in Felix Gonzalez-Torres, *(A.R.T.Press, 1993).*

Three poems by Jeremy Sigler

Carriage

Bar is flat
couch is fat

where I sit
I sat

away from
this and that

under
impact of
carriage age

carried cage
I flop
and flip

in start
and fit

feeling at
the force
of nothing

knowing
not to give

the underlive
away

Seacresea

Centered in
circle

of magnet
I miss

I knock and
shake unlock
and lift

luck called
to task

comes fast

but don't
ask how I
homed here

with
this herd
here in
buffalove

night knocks
its head

a pen impressed
with darkness

who heard
what wind
sin holes
in me

who peeps
through the
moon on me

who sees
this secrecy

this crawl
crashing
seacresea

Step On

Plank off ship
to dip onto
time to live

Plank you walk
the wall all
behind

Plank two sides
my sealed in
sights

Plank next
step please
step on

Jeremy Sigler is a poet and the Associate New York Editor of Parkett.

Now I See It . . .

I've had it happen when I was trying to fix the hay baler. To fix it, first you must figure out how it's supposed to work: this gear turns and then the twine fingers dip down just as the dog twists the twine over the hook. . . . It doesn't make sense until all of a sudden you visualize the whole motion and see the knot ties perfectly within your mind. Aha! The brain fairly explodes with the beauty and clarity of the vision. I can still tickle most of the vision back into my memory and experience an echo of that feeling of triumph.

But every farmer has had to figure out how a baler works and has had a similar experience. What of a discovery or creation of something never seen or understood before? Is it any different? Richard Feynman describes what it was like when he realized that he had broken through to the finish of his work with Murray Gell-Mann on weak interactions. It was not a triumphant feeling that he had made another significant discovery and would receive yet more honor; it was a calm and pleasant feeling that for that moment he knew something that no one else knew or ever had known. He was content with himself.

I recall working on an infinitely less significant physics problem. The equation that my colleague and I had developed looked awkward, wrong even—something about that denominator. I checked our work again and again; there was no error. Hmm. I tried inverting that pesky denominator, placing it in the numerator, and AHA! It was beautiful, it was correct, and suddenly I saw it all; the twine fingers dipped down. The work was done. But then there was that feeling, that I then knew something that no one else knew or had ever known. I was content with myself.

George Stranahan is a physicist, photographer, and social entrepreneur.

Dreams are beyond will, and you don't obtain anything by will once you cross the threshold of sleep. All facilities, all barriers change place: doors are walled up, and walls are made of gauze. There are known names on unknown people. What would make such things absurd is now asleep. It is absurd to walk on one's hands, but if one no longer has legs and if one has to move, such a thing is necessary.

Here, intimate mix of true and false. It is true that I am suffocating; it is false that a lion is pressing me. Something false (I created an opera) reminds me of something true (I don't know music). But not the whole of the true. Problem. It is the *inextricable* or the *indivisible* of this mix which is characteristic of the dream.

In the dream, I act without willing; I want without being able; I know without ever having seen, before having seen; I see without anticipating.

What is strange is not that functions are dispersed, it's that they come into play in this state.

The false or the arbitrary is the natural function of thought all alone. The notion of the true, of the real, implies a doubling. To think usefully, it is necessary, all at once, to confound the image with its object and be always be ready (*vigilare*)[1] to recognize that this apparent identity of very dissimilar things is only a provisional means, a use of the unfinished. It is because I confound them that I can think of acting, and because I do not confound them that I can act. The real is that from which one cannot wake up, that from which no movement pulls me, but that all movement reinforces, reproduces, regenerates. The non-real, on the contrary, is born in proportion to partial immobilization. (Observe that attention and sleep are not that far apart.) What is immobile engenders the false. Attention is not missing there when it exceeds a certain point.

In dreams, everything is equally imposed on me. When awake, I distinguish degrees of necessity and stability.

I dream of a perfume bottle in a purple box: I don't know who began. Is it the word "purple" or the coloration? There is symmetry in these members that substitute themselves one for the other. One is not more real than the other. If I look while awake at this flowered wallpaper, instead of an isotropic sowing of roses, I see only a group of parallel diagonals, and *I awaken* literally from this figure of choice, noticing that there are other equally possible figures in the field, with the help of the same elements.

Each of these figures is comparable to a dream; each is a complete and closed system, which suffices to entirely cover or mask the real multiplicity. The vision of one of these systems excludes the vision of the others.

In a tense milieu, undulating movements cross each other without combining. In the man awake, in some sense attuned to the real, there is, similarly, independence, not composition of coexisting excitations. In dreams, there is an automatic composition of everything, no reserve. If I think something about A, this judgment chases A away, since it is foreign to him. A judgment does not follow the impression in order to bring it into accord with a clear and uniform system that assures and defines my reality, my order. But this judgment follows my impression and cancels it entirely, or modifies it rather than consolidating it. One thinks as one bumps up against something.

To forget insensibly the thing that one is looking at. To forget it while thinking about it, by a natural, continuous, invisible, in plain daylight, immobile, local, imperceptible transformation... as a piece of glass escapes from the person who embraces it.

And inversely:

To find once more the forgotten thing by looking at the forgetting.

It often happens, if I have forgotten something precise, that I begin to observe myself to seize this state and this lacuna. I want to see myself forgetting, knowing that I have forgotten, and searching.

Maybe this is a method to oppose to all mental breakdown one's immediate study by conscience?

Thus (or contrarily?), even pain *pales*, for an instant, when one looks at it *head on*—if one can.

I forget that I have to go out tonight. I'm daydreaming of my slippers. But the beginning of the action makes me think of the well-being that will ensue, and this advance pleasure brings me to the pleasure of my intimate evening out. There, in this spiritual place in the future, something is already to be found: the place where I had to go awakens, with obligatory signs, and the remembered place refuses to receive my tranquil evening out. I remember the injunction, as a consequence of having forgotten it,--on account of having forgotten it with too much precision. Remember the injunction, as a consequence of having forgotten it,--on account of having forgotten it with too much precision.

I'm going to fall asleep, but a thread still holds within clear power, by which I can reciprocally hold it: a thread, a sensation still holding my whole being, and which can become a path for the waking state as well as for sleep.

Once asleep, I can no longer wake up voluntarily, I cannot see waking up as a goal. I have lost the vigor of looking at something as a dream.

It is necessary to wait for the fissure of day, the basement window that will deliver to me all my space, the connecting thread that brings back the state where efforts meet things, where sensation determines a common point between two visions. It is a double point belonging to an object and to my body all at once; to a thing, also to a knot of functions of mine.

In dreams, operations don't build themselves up, are not perceived as independent factors. There are sequences, not consequences. No goals, but the feeling of a goal. No object of thought forms by the manifest gathering of independent givens, so that it clearly owes its existence to a difference of "reality," to a finite machine. In the waking state, recognizing A is a phenomenon that depends on A, whereas in dreams I often recognize A in the object B. Recognition no longer results from a present shock: but it follows from the dream, as some kind of object contained in it.

The mind of the dreamer resembles a system on which external forces cancel themselves out or do not act, and of which the interior movements can bring neither movement from the center nor rotation.

One would not advance if the resistance of the ground and its friction did not come to cancel the force that tends to keep the center of gravity immobilized when the first leg moves away from the body. But if the back leg is asleep, the pressure on the ground does not awaken the stiffness or tension of the muscles, and the force is not cancelled, because the tension is not excited by the feeling of contact. One feels the ground as if from a distance, *as if in a dream*, without being able to answer.

And when the whole being is asleep, it is that the imprinted change or modification cannot bring a change or relative displacement, not that exterior forces are missing, but the instrument of their application is momentarily abolished.

The dreamer reacts by visions and movements that cannot change the cause of the impression. Unable to stop the impression by a partial, fixed image, unable to oppose such and such a (true) image to such and such a (false) one or to oppose memory to the present, etc., the dreamer is like someone who slides on a polished surface and who cannot *isolate* a leg by exterior fixation.

But the dreamer knows nothing about this. He takes even his inability for the effect of an exterior ability; he can never find the cause of his impressions to be finite, since he looks for it in the visions that the impression provokes; he looks for it by finding indefinitely, forging what can produce it rather than reproducing what produced it. He thinks he sees as he thinks he moves. But feelings, emotions, spectacles, apparent causes, simulacra of asides...modify each other reciprocally and constitute one and the same system, analogous to a system of "interior" forces. The effort that should produce a definite change remains always vain, because an inverse change, a sort of *moving back*, --moves me to the initial state, as a consequence of the very effort.

I wake up from a dream, and the object that I was holding tight, rope, becomes my other arm, in another world. The sensation of constriction still lasting, the cord I was grasping becomes animated. I have turned around a fixed point. The same sensation sort of illuminated and divided itself. The same stone enters into two successive constructions. The same bird walks to the edge of the roof, and, there, falls into flight.

I notice all of a sudden that it is necessary to translate this feeling in a completely different way: it's the moment that it can no longer belong to such a system of events, to such a *world*, that becomes *then* dream and unordered past.

Never does the dream reach this admirable *finite state* which perception attains in the waking state and in the light.

In such a dream is a character. But I do not see him distinctly. *For, if I saw him clearly, at that moment and as a result of that he would change*. There is conversation, but it is not distinct. I know well what we are discussing, and I hear certain words, but the continuation escapes me, no detail at all, and these words have no meaning: *(the Mellus of the Mellus??)* But nothing is missing. But everything happens as if the conversation were real. It is not stopped by its inconsistency. The motor is not in it.

In dreams thought does not distinguish itself from living and does not linger over it. Thought adheres to living; --it adheres entirely to the simplicity of living, to the fluctuation of the *being* under the faces and images of the *knowing*.

Paul Valéry (1871-1945) was a French poet, essayist, and philosopher.

Translated by Joseph Acquisto

This text was first published as the final section of Paul Valéry's Variété II *(Paris: Éditions Gallimard, 1930). It is translated here into English for the first time.*

[1]In Latin in the original. (trans.)

Walead Beshty, b. 1976

Walead Beshty was born in 1976 in London and currently lives and works in Los Angeles. Beshty holds a BA from Bard College (1999) and an MFA from Yale University School of Art (2002). Selected one-person exhibitions include *Science Concréte*, China Art Objects Galleries/Redling Fine Art, Los Angeles (2008); Galerie Rodolphe Janssen, Brussels, Belgium (2008); *The Grey Cloth*, Das Institut im Glaspavillon/Galerie Meerrettich, Berlin; *Hammer Project: Walead Beshty, EMBASSY!*, Hammer Museum, Los Angeles (2006); *The Maker and the Model*, Wallspace, New York (2006); and *The Phenomenology of Shopping and Dead Malls*, P.S.1 Contemporary Art Center, New York (2004). His work has been included in numerous group exhibitions, including the 2008 California Biennial, Orange County Museum of Art, Newport Beach; 2008 Whitney Biennial; *Word Event (After George Brecht)*, Kunsthalle Basel (2008); *Between Two Deaths*, ZKM Center for Art and Media, Karlsruhe, Germany (2007); and *Looking Back: The White Columns Annual*, White Columns, New York (2006).

Alexandra Bircken, b. 1967

Alexandra Bircken was born in 1967 in Cologne, Germany and lives and works in Cologne and London. She holds a BA (1995) and an MA (1997) in Fashion from Central Saint Martins College of Art and Design in London. Selected one-person exhibitions include *Units*, Docking Station, Stedelijk Museum, Amsterdam (2008); Gladstone Gallery, New York (2007), BQ, Cologne (2006), and Herald St., London (2005). Bircken's work has been shown in a number of group exhibitions, among them the 2008 Brussels Biennial; *Borders*, Museum Boijmans Van Beunigen, Rotterdam (2008); *Unmonumental*, New Museum of Contemporary Art, New York (2007); *Um-Kehrungen*, Kunstverein Braunschweig (2007); *Dereconstruction*, Gladstone Gallery, New York (2006); *Das Grosse Rasenstuck*, Outdoor Sculpture Project, Nuremberg (2006); and *Other People's Projects, Herald St.*, White Columns, New York (2005).

Ceal Floyer, b. 1968

Ceal Floyer was born in 1968 in Karachi, Pakistan and lives and works in Berlin. Floyer received her BA from Goldsmiths College, London (1994). Selected solo exhibitions include Museo d'Arte Contemporanea Donna Regina, Naples, Italy (2008); *Til I Get it Right*, Rochester Art Center, New York (2007); Museum Haus Esters, Krefeld, Germany (2007); Swiss Institute, New York (2006); Lisson Gallery, London (2006); and *MATRIX 192*, University of California, Berkeley Art Museum and Pacific Film Archive (2001). She has been included in numerous group exhibitions, including *50 Moons of Saturn*, 2nd Turin Triennial (2008); *...5 Minutes Later*, Kunst-Werke Institute for Contemporary Art, Berlin (2007); *Das Capital: Blue Chips and Masterpieces*, Museum für Moderne Kunst, Frankfurt (2007); the 2006 Shanghai Biennale; *5 Billion Years*, Palais de Tokyo, Paris (2006); *Material Matters*, Herbert F. Johnson Museum of Art, Ithaca, New York (2005); *Spiritus*, Magasin 3, Stockholm, Sweden (2003); *Liminal Space*, Center for Curatorial Studies, Bard College, New York (2002); and *Tempo*, The Museum of Modern Art, New York (2002).

Tom Friedman, b. 1965

Tom Friedman was born in St. Louis, Missouri in 1965, and currently lives and works in Conway, Massachusetts. He received his BFA at Washington University, St. Louis (1988) and his MFA at the University of Illinois at Chicago (1990). His recent one-person exhibitions include *Tom Friedman: Styrofoam*, Museum of Art, Rhode Island School of Design (2008); *Pure Invention: Tom Friedman*, Mildred Lane Kemper Art Museum, St Louis (2006). *Stitching*, Fondazione Prada, Milan (2002); and Fabric Workshop and Museum, Philadelphia (2001). In 2000, a mid-career retrospective of the artist's work was organized by the Southeastern Center for Contemporary Art, Winston-Salem, North Carolina, and traveled to the Museum of Contemporary Art, Chicago; Yerba Buena Center for the Arts, San Francisco; Aspen Art Museum; and the New Museum of Contemporary Art, New York. Friedman's recent group exhibitions include *All the More Real*, The Parrish Art Museum, Southampton, New York (2007), *The Shapes of Space*, Solomon R. Guggenheim Museum, New York (2007); *Into Me / Out of Me*, P.S.1 Contemporary Art Center, New York, travelled to Kunst-Werke Institute for Contemporary Art, Berlin (2006); and *A Brief History of Invisible Art*, CCA Wattis Institute for Contemporary Art, San Francisco (2005).

Felix Gonzalez-Torres (1957–1996)

Felix Gonzalez-Torres was born in Guáimaro, Cuba in 1957. He earned a BFA from Pratt Institute, New York (1983) and an MFA from the International Center of Photography and New York University (1987). His work has been included in innumerable international group exhibitions, and is part of numerous public collections throughout the world. Comprehensive retrospective exhibitions of Gonzalez-Torres's work have been organized by the Museum of Contemporary Art in Los Angeles (1994), Solomon R. Guggenheim Museum (1995), Springer Museum Hannover (1997), and Banco de la República, Biblioteca Luis Ángel Arango in Bogotá (2000). In 2007, he was selected to represent the United States at the 53rd Venice Biennale. He died in Miami, Florida on January 9, 1996.

Wade Guyton, b. 1972

Wade Guyton was born in 1972 in Hammond, Indiana and lives and works in New York. He received his BA from the University of Tennessee (1995) and MFA from Hunter College, New York (1998). Selected one-person exhibitions include Portikus, Frankfurt (2008); LA><ART, Los Angeles (2008); *Guyton\Walker: Empire Strikes Back*, Carpenter Center, Harvard University, Cambridge (2006); *Color, Power & Style*, Kunstverein Hamburg (2005); and *Elements of an Incomplete Map*, Artists Space, New York (2003). Guyton's work has been included in numerous recent group exhibitions, including *Oranges and Sardines: Conversations on Abstract Painting*, Hammer Museum, Los Angeles (2008); *Records Played Backwards*, Modern Institute, Glasgow (2008); the 2007 Lyon Biennale, Museum of Contemporary Art, Lyon; *What is Painting?*, Museum of Modern Art, New York (2007); *Greater New York*, P.S.1 Contemporary Art Center, New York (2005), and the 2004 Whitney Biennial.

Wolfgang Laib, b. 1950

Wolfgang Laib was born in Metzingen, Germany in 1950 and lives and works in southern Germany. He received his medical degree in 1974 from the University of Tübingen and began working exclusively as an artist soon after. In 2000, a restrospective of his work was organized by the Hirshhorn Museum and Sculpture Garden, Washington, D.C., and traveled to the Henry Art Gallery, Seattle; Dallas Museum of Art; Scottsdale Museum of Contemporary Art; Museum of Contemporarty Art, San Diego; and Haus der Kunst, Munich. His recent exhibitions include Auckland Art Gallery, Auckland, New Zealand (2006); Fondation Beyeler, Basel, Switzerland, (2006); Museo d'Arte Contemporanea Roma, Rome (2006); and *Wolfgang Laib—Passageway—Overgoing*, Guangdong Museum of Art, Guangzhou, China (2004).

Robert Morris, b. 1931

Robert Morris was born in 1931 in Kansas City, and currently lives and works in New York City and Gardiner, New York. Morris studied at the Kansas City Art Institute and the University of Kansas (1948–1950), the California School of Fine Arts in San Francisco (1951), and Hunter College (1962) and taught Art History at Hunter College beginning in 1964. Numerous museums have organized solo exhibitions of his work, including New York's Whitney Museum of American Art (1970), the Art Institute of Chicago (1980), the Museum of Contemporary Art, Chicago (1986), and Corcoran Gallery of Art, Washington, D.C. (1990). In 1994, the Solomon R. Guggenheim Museum, New York, organized a major retrospective of the artist's work, which traveled to the Deichtorhallen in Hamburg and the Musée National d'Art Moderne in Paris.

William J. O'Brien, b. 1975

William O'Brien was born in 1975 in Cleveland and currently lives and works in Chicago. He received his BA from Loyola University, Chicago (1997) and his MFA from The School of the Art Institute of Chicago (2005). Selected exhibitions include *Sonotube® Forms: Contemporary Art and Transport*, Santa Barbara Contemporary Arts Forum, Santa Barbara (2007); *the axis mundi*, Shane Campbell Gallery, Chicago (2007); *When Your Heart Is on Fire, Smoke Gets in Your Eyes*, Locust Projects, Miami (2006); and 12 x 12, *New Artists, New Work*, Museum of Contemporary Art, Chicago (2005).

Mitzi Pederson, b. 1976

Mitzi Pederson was born in Stuart, Florida in 1976, and currently lives and works in San Francisco. She received her BFA from Carnegie Mellon University, Pittsburgh (1999) and her MFA from the California College of the Arts, San Francisco (2004). Selected solo exhibitions include Hammer Museum, Los Angeles (2008); Ratio 3, San Francisco (2007); Nicole Klagsbrun Gallery, New York (2007); and White Columns, New York (2006). Group exhibitions of her work include the 2008 Whitney Biennial; the 2006 SECA Art Award Exhibition, San Francisco Museum of Modern Art; *Five Habitats: Squatting at Langton*, New Langton Arts, San Francisco (2006), and *Louis Morris*, Atlanta Contemporary Art Center (2006).

Dieter Roth (1930–1998)

Dieter Roth was born in 1930 in Hanover, Germany. He was a graphic design apprentice at Bern from 1947–1951 and began making experimental works incorporating materials subject to decomposition in 1954. He lived in the US from 1964–1967 and taught at Yale University. Roth has been exhibited extensively throughout the world, with recent one-person exhibitions at MACBA, Barcelona (2001); Staatsgalerie, Stuttgart (2001); Secession, Vienna (1995); and the Living Art Museum, Reykjavík (1994). In 2004, the Museum of Modern Art, New York organized a major retrospective of the artist's work, *Roth Time: A Dieter Roth Retrospective*, which traveled to the Schaulager, Basel, and the Museum Ludwig, Cologne. Roth died in Basel, Switzerland in 1998.

Robert Ryman, b. 1930

Robert Ryman was born in Nashville, Tennessee (1930) and lives and works in New York. Ryman studied at the Tennessee Polytechnic Institute and the George Peabody College for Teachers, Nashville, before serving in the United States Army (1950-52). Ryman's work has been the subject of numerous one-person museum exhibitions, including a 1993-94 international, traveling retrospective jointly organized by the Tate Gallery, London, and the Museum of Modern Art, New York, whose venues also included the Museo Nacional Centro de Arte Reina Sofia, Madrid; The San Francisco Museum of Modern Art; and the Walker Art Center, Minneapolis. In 2001, the Haus der Kunst, Munich, organized *Robert Ryman Retrospective*, which traveled to the Kunstmuseum Bonn. Ryman's work has been included in Documentas 5, 6, and 7 (1872-82); the Venice Biennale in 1976, 1978, and 1980; the Whitney Biennial in 1977, 1987, and 1995; and the 50th Carnegie International, Pittsburgh (1988).

Fred Sandback, b. 1943

Fred Sandback was born in Bronxville, New York (1943). He received his BA from Yale University (1966) and his MFA from the Yale University School of Art and Architecture (1969). Since the late sixties, Sandback has exhibited widely in museums both in the United States and abroad. Recent one-person exhibitions include the Musée de Grenoble, Grenoble, France (2007); *Fred Sandback: Frühe Skulpturen*, Metropol Kunstraum, Munich (2007); *Fred Sandback: Early Work*, Zwirner & Wirth, New York (2006); Dia:Beacon, New York (2003); and Museo Tamayo, Mexico City (2002).

Anna Sew Hoy, b. 1976

Anna Sew Hoy was born in Auckland, New Zealand in 1976 and lives and works in Los Angeles and New York. She received her BFA from the School of Visual Arts in New York (1998) and her MFA from Hunter College in New York (2001). Selected solo exhibitions include LA><ART, Los Angeles (2008); Karyn Lovegrove Gallery, Los Angeles (2007); *Broken Arm*, Peres Projects, Los Angeles (2003), and *Wash My Bike*, Massimo Audiello Gallery, New York. Recent group exhibitions include Eden's Edge, Hammer Museum, Los Angeles (2007); *Cosmic Wonder*, Yerba Buena Center for the Arts, San Francisco (2006); *One Way or Another*, Asia Society, New York (2006), *Diamond Hand Grenade*, Midway Contemporary Art, Minneapolis; and *i and i and i and i*, Locust Projects, Miami (2004).

Gedi Sibony, b. 1973

Gedi Sibony was born in New York in 1973, where he continues to live and work. He received his BA from Brown University in Providence (1995) and his MFA from Columbia University (2000). Selected one-person exhibitions include FRAC Champagne-Ardenne, Reims, France (2008); *If Surrounded by Foxes*, Kunsthalle St. Gallen, Switzerland (2007); *The Science of Imaginary Solutions*, Midway Contemporary Art, Minneapolis (2007); Galerie Art: Concept, Paris (2006); and The Wrong Gallery, New York (2005). Selected group exhibitions include *Unmonumental*, The New Museum of Contemporary Art, New York (2007); The 2006 Whitney Biennial; *Greater New York*, P.S.1 Contemporary Art Center, New York (2005); *Summer Selections*, The Drawing Center, New York (2004); and *Breaking Ground*, White Columns, New York (2003).

Rudolf Stingel, b. 1956

Rudolf Stingel was born in 1956 in Merano, Italy and currently lives and works in New York. Selected solo exhibitions include *Rudolf Stingel: Paintings 1987-2007*, Museum of Contemporary Art, Chicago, which traveled to the Whitney Museum of American Art, New York (2007); *Plan B*, Walker Art Center, Minneapolis (2004); *Home Depot*, Museum für Moderne Kunst, Frankfurt (2004); and Museo di Arte Moderna e Contemporanea, Palazzo delle Arbere, Trento, Italy (2001). His work has been included in numerous international group exhibitions, including *Sequence 1: Painting and Sculpture from the Francois Pinault Collection*, Palazzo Grassi, Venice (2007); *Infinite Painting: Contemporary Painting and Global Realism*, Villa Manin Center for Contemporary Art, Passariano, Italy (2006); the 2006 Whitney Biennial; *Universal Experience: Art, Life, and the Tourist's Eye*, Museum of Contemporary Art Chicago (2005); and *None of the Above*, Swiss Institute, New York (2004).

Lawrence Weiner, b. 1942

Lawrence Weiner was born in 1942, in the Bronx, New York, and currently lives and works in New York and Amsterdam. Solo exhibitions of the artist's work have been mounted at the Hirshhorn Museum and Sculpture Garden, Washington, D.C. (1990), Institute of Contemporary Arts, London (1991), Dia Center for the Arts, New York (1991), Musée d'Art Contemporain, Bordeaux (1991 and 1992), San Francisco Museum of Modern Art (1992), Walker Art Center, Minneapolis (1994), Philadelphia Museum of Art (1994), and Museum Ludwig, Cologne (1995). In 2007, the first major retrospective of the artist's work, *Lawrence Weiner: AS FAR AS THE EYE CAN SEE*, was jointly organized by The Museum of Contemporary Art, Los Angeles, and the Whitney Museum of American Art, New York.

Jennifer West, b. 1969

Jennifer West was born in 1969 in Topanga Canyon, California, and currently lives and works in Los Angeles. She received her MFA from the Art Center College of Design in Pasadena, California (2004). Selected solo exhibitions include Vilma Gold, London (2008); *Lemon Juice and Lithium*, Transmission Gallery, Glasgow (2008); White Columns, New York (2007); and MARC FOXX (2007). Group exhibitions include *ARTLV 08*, Tel Aviv Museum of Art, Tel Aviv (2008); *here's why patterns*, Misako and Rosen, Toyko (2008); *Drawing on Film*, Drawing Center, New York, traveling to The Rose Art Museum, Waltham, Massachusetts (2008); *When Words Fail*, Contemporary Art Museum, Detroit, Michigan (2007); and *Between Two Deaths*, ZKM Center for Art and Media, Karlsruhe, Germany (2007).

Erwin Wurm, b. 1954

Erwin Wurm was born in 1954 in Bruck, Austria, and currently lives and works in Vienna and New York. He attended the Academy of Applied Arts, Vienna and Academy of Fine Arts, Vienna from 1979 to 1982. Recent solo exhibitions include Deichtorhallen Hamburg, Hamburg, Germany (2007); Kunstmuseum St. Gallen, Switzerland (2007); Musee d'Art Contemporain Lyon, France (2007); *I Love My Time, I Don't Like My Time*, Yerba Bunea Center for the Arts, San Francisco, traveling to the Contemporary Art Center Cincinnati (2005); ZKM Center for Art and Media, Karlsruhe, Germany (2003) and *Erwin Wurm: Videos*, Rhode Island School of Design, Providence, Rhode Island (2003). Wurm's work has been included in numerous international group exhibitions, including recently *Affinities–Deutsche Guggenheim, 1997-2007*, Deutsche Guggenheim, Berlin (2007); *All About Laughter: Humor in Contemporary Art*, Mori Art Museum, Tokyo (2007); the 2004 Seville International Biennial of Contemporary Art, Seville, Spain; and *Work Ethic*, Baltimore Museum of Art, which traveled to the Des Moines Art Center, Des Moines, Iowa; and the Wexner Center for the Arts, Columbus, Ohio (2003).

Exhibition Checklist

Walead Beshty

Fold (80 degree directional light source) November 27th, 2006, Valencia, CA, Ilford, Multigrade fiber IV, 2007
Black-and-white photogram on fiber-based gelatin silver paper
93 1/2 x 51 1/2 inches
Collection of Jann and Kenneth Williams

Fold (Three Directional Light Sources, 35/62.5/145 degrees), December 22nd, 2006, Valencia, CA, Ilford Multigrade Fiber IV, 2007
Black-and-white photogram on fiber-based gelatin silver paper
100 1/2 x 55 inches
Courtesy of the artist and Wallspace, New York

Alexandra Bircken

Ship, 2007
Branches, dried plants, wool, and copper wire
60 5/8 x 56 3/8 x 40 1/2 inches
Private Collection, Boston

Spindel, 2007
Branches, wool, and copper wire
96 x 44 x 27 inches
Courtesy of Martin and Rebecca Eisenberg

Ceal Floyer

Door, 1999
35 mm metal mask slide, slide projector
Dimensions variable
Courtesy of 303 Gallery New York, Lisson Gallery, London, and Esther Schipper, Berlin

Ink on Paper (video), 1999
Video, color, silent
51:53
Ed. 1/3
Courtesy of 303 Gallery New York, Lisson Gallery, London, and Esther Schipper, Berlin

Tom Friedman

Two by Four, 1990
Acrylic on wood
48 x 3 3/4 x 1 3/4 inches
Courtesy of Robert and Nancy Magoon

1,000 Hours of Staring, 1997
Stare on paper
32 1/4 x 32 1/2 inches
The Museum of Modern Art, New York. Gift of Dean Valentine and Amy Adelson, 2008

Felix Gonzalez-Torres

"Untitled" (Last Light), 1993
10-watt light bulbs, extension cord, plastic light sockets, and dimmer switch
Dimensions variable
Courtesy of Robert and Nancy Magoon
© The Felix Gonzalez-Torres Foundation, Courtesy Andrea Rosen Gallery

"Untitled" (Water), 1995
Plastic beads and metal rod
Installation dimensions variable
© The Felix Gonzalez-Torres Foundation, Courtesy Andrea Rosen Gallery

Wade Guyton

Untitled, 2007
Epson UltraChrome inkjet on linen
84 x 69 inches
Courtesy of Warren and Allison Kanders

Anna Sew Hoy

Heart, 2007
Ceramic, chain, denim, resin, and screw
60 x 20 1/2 x 4 inches
Courtesy of the artist and Karyn Lovegrove Gallery

Two Eyes, 2007
Glazed ceramic, chain, denim, resin, and screw
75 x 17 1/2 x 5 inches
Courtesy of the artist and Karyn Lovegrove Gallery

Wolfgang Laib

Milkstone, 1997
Marble
2 3/8 x 14 9/16 x 11 7/16 inches
Courtesy of Jeanne and Michael Klein

Robert Morris

Vetti V, 1993
Felt
98 x 137 x 39 inches
Courtesy of Debra and Dennis Scholl, Miami Beach, FL

William O'Brien

Untitled, 2008
Glazed ceramic, wood, paint, acrylic, hardware, and mixed media
70 x 11 1/4 x 11 1/4 inches
Courtesy of Debra and Dennis Scholl, Miami Beach, FL

Untitled, 2008
Glazed ceramic, enamel, plaster, table, and ink on paper
88 1/2 x 72 1/2 x 55 inches
Courtesy of Shane Campbell Gallery, Chicago, and Marianne Boesky Gallery, New York

Mitzi Pederson

Untitled, 2008
Wood and silver leaf
28 x 6 1/2 x 3 1/2 inches
Courtesy of Miller Meigs Collection

Untitled, 2008
Cinderblock, wood, sand, glue, and string
59 x 8 x 8 inches
Courtesy of Yves Behar

Dieter Roth

Lion Bust, 1961
Sugar, food coloring, and acrylic paint
9 x 6 x 7 inches
Courtesy of Ira G. Wool and Barbara Mirecki

Schokoladenplätzchenbild (chocolate wafer picture), 1969
Chocolate wafers and curdled milk in plastic
20 1/2 x 28 1/4 x 1 1/4 inches
Courtesy of Ira G. Wool and Barbara Mirecki

Schokoladenlowe, 1969–89
Chocolate
9 3/4 x 5 3/4 x 7 inches
Private Collection

Robert Ryman

Untitled, 1961
Oil paint and gesso on unstretched linen canvas
14 x 14 inches
Anonymous Collection

Series #22 (White), 2004
Oil on canvas
16 x 16 inches
Courtesy of Susan and Larry Marx

Fred Sandback

Untitled (Sculptural Study, Two-part Leaning Construction), 1977/2004
Orange and black acrylic yarn
108 x 6 x 14 inches
Estate of Fred Sandback, Courtesy of Zwirner & Wirth, New York

Gedi Sibony

Left So Soon, 2008
Carpet
95 1/2 x 33 inches
Private Collection, New York

The Last One, 2008
Hollow-core door, garbage bags, and tape
88 x 29 x 3 inches
Courtesy of Laura Steinberg and B. Nadal-Ginard

Rudolf Stingel

Untitled, 2002
Celotex insulation board, wood, and aluminum
94 1/4 x 95 1/8 inches
Collection of Frances Dittmer

Lawrence Weiner

A 36" X 36" REMOVAL TO THE LATHING OR SUPPORT WALL OF PLASTER OR WALLBOARD FROM A WALL, 1968
36 x 36 inches
Courtesy of the Sieglaub Collection & Archives at the Stichting Egress Foundation, Amsterdam

Jennifer West

Green M&M's and Mezcal Worm Film (70 mm film leader with a mescal worm dragged over the surface – imprinted with hundreds of green M & Ms), 2008
DVD transferred from 70 mm film, no sound
Courtesy of the artist and Marc Foxx, Los Angeles

Electric Kool-Aid Fountain Swimming Film (35 mm movie negative submerged in LA's Mulholland Fountain, dripped with Kool-Aid and liquid LSD – featuring nighttime fountain swimming by Mateo Tannatt, Lia Trinka-Brownwe, Lesley Moon, Mariah Csepanyi and Jwest), 2008
DVD transferred from 35 mm film, no sound
Courtesy of the artist and Marc Foxx, Los Angeles

Erwin Wurm

Dust Piece, 1991
Wood, glass, paint, and dust
49 x 12 1/2 x 18 inches
Courtesy of Jack Hanley

Untitled (Dust Piece), 1991
Wood platform, pedestal, and dust
6 x 19 1/2 x 55 1/2 inches
Courtesy of Jack Hanley

Lenders to the Exhibition

303 Gallery, New York
Amy Adelson
Baltimore Museum of Art
Yves Behar
Frances Dittmer
Martin and Rebecca Eisenberg
Esther Schipper, Berlin
Jack Hanley
Warren and Allison Kanders
Karyn Lovegrove Gallery
Jeanne and Michael Klein
Lisson Gallery, London
Robert and Nancy Magoon
Marc Foxx, Los Angeles
Marianne Boesky Gallery, New York
Susan and Larry Marx
Miller Meigs
Museum of Modern Art, New York
Debra and Dennis Scholl
Shane Cambell Gallery, Chicago
Siegelaub Collection & Archives at
the Stichting Egress Foundation, Amsterdam
Laura Steinberg and B. Nadal–Ginard
Wallspace, New York
Ira G. Wool and Barbara Mirecki
Jann and Kenneth Williams
Zwirner & Wirth, New York
Private Collections

List of Illustrations

[Page 6] Ad Reinhardt, *Abstract Painting*, 1960-61. Digital Image © The Museum of Modern Art / Licensed by SCALA / Art Resources, New York. © 2008 Estate of Ad Reinhardt / Artist Rights Society (ARS), New York.

[Page 9] Kurt Schwitters, *Mz 129 rot oben [Mz 129 Red on top]*, 1920. © 2008 Artists Rights Society (ARS), New York / VG Bild-Kunst, Bonn.

[Page 10] Bruce Nauman, *Pay Attention Mother Fuckers*, 1973. © 1973 Bruce Nauman and Gemini G.E.L. / Artist Rights Society (ARS), New York.

[Page 11] Bruce Nauman, *The True Artist Helps the World by Revealing Mystic Truths (Window or Wall Sign)*, 1967. © 2008 Bruce Nauman / Artist Rights Society (ARS), New York . Courtesy Sperone Westwater, New York. Philadelphia Museum of Art: Purchased with the Henry P. McIlhenny Fund, the bequest (by exchange) of Henrietta Meyers Miller, the gift (by exchange) of Philip L. Goodwin, and contributions from generous donors, 2007.

[Page 13] Bruce Nauman, *John Coltane Piece*, 1968. © 2008 Bruce Nauman / Artist Rights Society (ARS), New York.

[Page 14] Bruce Nauman, *Failing to Levitate in the Studio*, 1966. Collection of the artist. Courtesy Sperone Westwater, New York. © 2008 Bruce Nauman / Artist Rights Society (ARS), New York.

[Page 15] Ceal Floyer, *Light*, 1994. Installation view, "British Art Show 4", Manchester / Edinburgh / Cardiff, 1995 Courtesy of 303 Gallery, New York; Lisson Gallery, London; Esther Schipper Berlin.

[Page 16] Robert Rauschenberg, *Erased de Kooning Drawing*, 1953. San Francisco Museum of Modern Art. Purchased through a gift of Phyllis Wattis. © Estate of Robert Rauschenberg / Licensed by VAGA, New York, NY.

[Page 18 – 19] Wade Guyton, *Untitled*, 2007. Image courtesy of Friedrich Petzel Gallery, New York.

[Page 20 – 21] Robert Ryman, *Untitled*, 1961. © Robert Ryman, Courtesy PaceWildenstein, New York.

[Page 22 – 23] Robert Ryman, *Series #22 (White)*, 2004. © Robert Ryman, Courtesy PaceWildenstein, New York.

[Page 24 – 25] Walead Beshty, *Fold (Three Directional Light Sources, 35/62.5/145 degrees), December 22nd, 2006, Valencia, CA, Ilford Multigrade Fiber IV*, 2008. Image courtesy of the artist and Wallspace, New York.

[Page 26 – 27] Walead Beshty, *Fold (80 degree directional light source) November 27th, Valencia, CA, Ilford, Multigrade fiber IV*, 2007. Image courtesy of the artist and Wallspace, New York.

[Page 28 – 29] Gedi Sibony, *The Last One*, 2008. Image courtesy of Greene Naftali Gallery, New York.

[Page 30 – 31] Gedi Sibony, *Left So Soon*, 2008. Image courtesy of Greene Naftali Gallery, New York.

[Page 32 – 33] Robert Morris, *Vetti V*, 1983. Image courtesy of Sonnabend Gallery © 2008 Robert Morris / Artist Rights Society (ARS), New York.

[Page 34 – 35] Lawrence Weiner, *A 36" X 36" REMOVAL TO THE LATHING OR SUPPORT WALL OF A PLASTER OR WALLBOARD FROM A WALL*, 1968. Installation view at Pocket Utopia, Brooklyn, 2007 (photograph by James Wagner of jameswagner.com). Courtesy of the Siegelaub Collection & Archives at the Stichting Egress Foundation, Amsterdam. © 2008 Lawrence Weiner / Artists Rights Society (ARS), New York.

[Page 36 – 37] Fred Sandback, *Untitled (Sculptural Study, Two-part Leaning Construction)*, 1977 / 2004. Estate of Fred Sandback, Courtesy of Zwirner & Wirth, New York. Photography by Ben Cohen.

[Page 38 – 39] Ceal Floyer, *Door*, 1995. Image courtesy of 303 Gallery, New York.

[Page 40 – 41] Ceal Floyer, *Ink on Paper (video)*, 1999. Image courtesy of 303 Gallery, New York.

[Page 42 – 43] Tom Friedman, *1,000 Hours of Staring*, 1992-97. © Tom Friedman. Courtesy Gagosian Gallery. Gift of Dean Valentine and Amy Adelson. The Museum of Modern Art, New York, NY, U.S.A.

[Page 44 – 45] Tom Friedman, *Two by Four*, 1990. © Tom Friedman. Courtesy Gagosian Gallery.

[Page 46 – 47] Jennifer West, *Electric Kool-Aid Fountain Swimming Film (35MM movie negative submerged in LA's Mulholland Fountain, dripped with Kool-aid and liquid LSD – featuring nighttime fountain swimming by Mateo Tannatt, Lia Trinka-Browner, Lesley Moon, Mariah Csepanyi and Jwest)*, 2008.
Courtesy of the artist and Marc Foxx, Los Angeles.

[Page 48 – 49] Jennifer West, *Green M&M's & Mezcal Worm Film (70MM film leader with a mescal worm dragged over the surface – imprinted with hundreds of green M&M's)*, 2008. Courtesy of the artist and Marc Foxx, Los Angeles.

[Page 50 – 51] Erwin Wurm, *Dust Piece*, 1991.
© 2008 Artists Rights Society (ARS), New York / VBK, Vienna.

[Page 52 – 53] Erwin Wurm, *Untitled (Dust Piece)*, 1991.
© 2008 Artists Rights Society (ARS), New York / VBK, Vienna.

[Page 54 – 55] Rudolf Stingel, *Untitled*, 2002. © R. Stingel. Image courtesy of Paula Cooper Gallery, New York. RS-189-PTG Photographed by Adam Reich.

[Page 56 – 57] Wolfgang Laib, *Milkstone*, 1997.
Image courtesy Sperone Westwater, New York.

[Page 58 – 59] Felix Gonzalez –Torres, *"Untitled" (Last Light)*, 1993.
© The Felix Gonzalez-Torres Foundation, Courtesy Andrea Rosen Gallery.

[Page 60 – 61] Felix Gonzalez –Torres, *"Untitled" (Water)*, 1995.
© The Felix Gonzalez-Torres Foundation, Courtesy Andrea Rosen Gallery.

[Page 62 – 63] Dieter Roth, *Lion Bust*, 1993.
© Dieter Roth estate. Photographed by Julita Siegel.

[Page 64 – 65] Dieter Roth, *Schokoladenplätzchenbild (Chocolate wafer picture)*, 1969.
© Dieter Roth estate. Photographed by Julita Siegel.

[Page 66 – 67] Dieter Roth, *Schokoladenlowe*, 1969-89.
© Dieter Roth estate. Photographed by Dr. Dirk Dobke.

[Page 68 – 69] Alexandra Bircken, *Ship*, 2007.
©Alexandra Bircken. Image courtesy of Gladstone Gallery.

[Page 70 – 71] Alexandra Bircken, *Spindel*, 2007.
©Alexandra Bircken. Image courtesy Gladstone Gallery.

[Page 72 – 73] Anna Sew Hoy, *Heart*, 2007.
Image courtesy of the artist and Karyn Lovegrove Gallery.

[Page 74 – 75] Anna Sew Hoy, *Two Eyes*, 2007.
Image courtesy of the artist and Karyn Lovegrove Gallery.

[Page 76 – 77] Mitzi Pederson, *Untitled*, 2008. Image courtesy of Ratio3, San Francisco.

[Page 78 – 79] Mitzi Pederson, *Untitled*, 2008. Image courtesy of Ratio3, San Francisco.

[Page 80 – 81] William O'Brien, *Untitled*, 2008. Image courtesy of the artist, Shane Campbell Gallery, Chicago, and Marianne Boesky Gallery, New York.

[Page 82 – 83] William O'Brien, *Untitled*, 2008. Image courtesy of the artist, Shane Campbell Gallery, Chicago, and Marianne Boesky Gallery, New York.
Photographed by Tom Van Eynde.

Museum Staff

Heidi Zuckerman Jacobson
Director and Chief Curator

Karyn Andrade
Visitor Services Assistant

Dasa Bausova
Visitor Services Assistant

Dale Benson
Chief Preparator and Facilities Manager

Grace Brooks
Campaign Coordinator

Rich Cieciuch
Project Manager

Ellie Closuit
Membership Assistant

Dara Coder
Assistant Director for Finance and Administration

Nicole Kinsler
Curatorial Associate

Giselle Leal
Interim Education and Public Programs Coordinator

Lauren Lively
Executive Assistant to the Director

Jeff Murcko
Public Relations and Marketing Manager

Jared Rippy
Graphic Designer

Rachel Rippy
Web and Graphic Design Associate

Christy Sauer
Assistant Development Director

John-Paul Schaefer
Assistant Director for External Affairs

Dorie Schellenbergar
Visitor Services Coordinator

Pam Taylor
Registrar and Exhibitions Manager

Matthew Thompson
Associate Curator

Wendy Wilhelm
Special Events Assistant

Karl Wolfgang
Staff Photographer

Now You See It
December 18, 2008–February 1, 2009
Aspen Art Museum

590 North Mill Street, Aspen, CO 81611
aspenartmuseum.org

Library of Congress Control Number 2008938030
ISBN 9780934324441

Texts by Heidi Zuckerman Jacobson, Peter Eleey, Jeremy Sigler, George Stranahan, and Paul Valéry

Catalogue design by Jared Rippy

Edited by Richard Slovak

Published by Aspen Art Press

Printed by Perry/Granger & Associates San Francisco

Printed and bound in the United States

Available through D.A.P./Distributed Art Publishers
155 Sixth Avenue, 2nd Floor, New York, N.Y. 10013
Tel: (212) 627-1999 Fax: (212) 627-9484

The AAM presentation of *Now You See It* is organized by the Aspen Art Museum and funded in part by the AAM National Council. AAM Art Talks are part of the Questrom Lecture Series.

Generous underwriting is also provided by Susan and Larry Marx.